FORTY DAYS ON LOVE

By

Jason Pullen

To know Love is to know God.

Love never fails. God is Love

Book #7 from the series 40 Days with God by Jason Pullen

CONTENTS

Heading	Page
Dedication & Acknowledgements	3
Salvation Prayer	5
Introduction	6
Love Explained	10
God's Love, Natural Love & Wrong "love" – Day 1	18
God Loved You First – Day 2	25
Mercy Triggers Love – Day 3	28
Love Yourself – Day 4	32
Love Fulfills The Law – Day 5	41
The Love Of God In Your Heart – Day 6	46
A New Commandment – Day 7	50
Love Covers A Multitude Of sins – Day 8	53
From death To Life Because Of Love – Day 9	58
To Love Is To Know God – Day 10	65
Constrained By Love – Day 11	70
Faith Works By Love – Day 12	75
The Debt Of Love – Day 13	79
Love The Fruit – Day 14	83
Labour Of Love – Day 15	88
Prove Your Love – Day 16	94
Love Rebukes & Corrects – Day 17	100
The Jealousy Of Love – Day 18	107
Love Gives Meaning – Day 19	113
Love Is A Fire – Day 20	118
Love Is Patient – Day 21	125
Love Is Kind – Day 22	128
Love Does Not Envy – Day 23	132

Love Is Not Proud – Day 24	138
Love Is Not Rude – Day 25	145
Love Is Not Self-Seeking – Day 26	151
Love Is Not Easily Provoked – Day 27	155
Love Thinks No evil – Day 28	159
Love Rejoices Not In Iniquity – Day 29	164
Love Rejoices In The Truth – Day 30	167
Love Bears All Things – Day 31	171
Love Believes All Things – Day 32	176
Love Hopes All Things – Day 33	178
Love Endures All Things – Day 34	181
Love Never Fails – Day 35	185
Love Versus fear – Day 36	188
Love God Not Money – Day 37	193
Love Is The Greatest – Day 38	198
Love Is Perfection – Day 39	202
God Is Love – Day 40	207
Conclusion	210

Dedication

- This book is dedicated to the Lord Jesus Christ and His Kingdom. For counting me faithful and by His Power making my hand the pen of a ready writer I thank you Jesus!
- To the beloved children of God who want to know Him.
- To those who have been deceived and want to genuinely know what Love is.

Forty Days On Love 1ˢᵗ Edition 2024
© Copyright 2024 – Jason Pullen
The Word Of Truth
All rights reserved. This book is protected by copyright law. Published by The Word Of Truth Publications. For Worldwide distribution. The use of short quotations, discussion and study is encouraged. Writings may be shared with accreditation to the copyright holder. They may not be modified in any way. This work and the parts thereof may not be reproduced or modified in any form, including photocopy, for internal use or sale without written permission from the copyright holder.

Unless otherwise stated all Scripture quotations are taken from the King James Version of the bible (KJV).
New King James Version (NKJV), Modern King James Version (MKJV), King James 2000 (KJ2000), The Net Bible (NET), New International Version (NIV), New Living Translation (NLT), New Life Version 1968 (NLV), Message Bible (MSG), A Conservative Version (ACV), Amplified Bible (AMP), Bible In Basic English (BBE), Complete Apostle's Bible (CAB), Good News Bible (GNB), God's Word Bible (GW), Complete Jewish Bible (CJB), New Century Version (NCV), New International Readers Version (NIRV)

Strong's Hebrew & Greek Dictionaries

(Bold & Italic texts are for emphasis by the author)

All rights reserved to the above mentioned Copyright Holders.

Forty Days On Love 1ˢᵗ Edition 2024
ISBN NUMBER; 978-1-77924-266-2
EAN NUMBER; 9781779242662

Web; https://www.facebook.com/FortyDaysOnLove
For additional information contact the publisher

Email; thewordoftruthpublications@gmail.com
Web; https://thewordoftruthjc.blogspot.com
https://www.facebook.com/TheWordOfTruthJC
https://www.instagram.com/TheWordOfTruthJC
https://twitter.com/TheWordOf_Truth @TheWordOf_Truth
https://www.youtube.com/@thewordoftruthjasonpaulpullen

Contact the Author

Email; jaycep@hotmail.com
Other Writings by the Author Now That You Are Saved, New Believers' Foundation, Forty Days On Salvation, Forty days On Grace, Forty days on Mercy, Forty Days on Righteousness, Forty Days on Faith, Forty Days on Hope, The Word For Today Devotions
Web; https://www.facebook.com/NowThatYouRSaved
Web; https://www.facebook.com/NewBelieversFoundation
Web; https://www.facebook.com/FortyDaysOnSalvation
Web; https://www.facebook.com/FortyDaysOnGrace
Web; https://www.facebook.com/FortyDaysOnMercy
Web; https://www.facebook.com/FortyDaysOnRighteousness
Web; https://www.facebook.com/FortyDaysOnFaith
Web; https://www.facebook.com/FortyDaysOnHope

Cover design by

Real Deal Graphic Designs
Email; realdealgraphicdesigns@gmail.com

Acknowledgements

I would like to acknowledge my Heavenly Father for giving me the wisdom, revelation and ability to write this book as He told me. It is all because of His Love for me that this book and this series have been made possible.

May all the Glory go to the Lord Jesus Christ.

Salvation Prayer

Lord Jesus come into my life and be the Lord of my life. I believe that you died for me and rose from the dead. I receive forgiveness for all my sins. I declare that I am saved I am born again. I am filled with the Holy Spirit and washed in the blood of Jesus. In Jesus name. Amen

If you have just prayed this prayer congratulations now starts the beginning of your life in Christ. As we go through these forty days we will get deeper in understanding what you now have access to having received Salvation in Jesus Christ.

FORTY DAYS ON LOVE

INTRODUCTION

Welcome reader to this forty day devotion on Love. This is part in a series of daily devotions by the author Jason Pullen. You are advised to read the previous six books in this series first before this one on Love. That way you will truly receive what this book contains. Take your time to meditate on the verses, devotions and say out the confessions or prayers to enjoy the full experience from these devotions.

Let's pause and think on the scripture below:

Daniel answered and said, Blessed be the name of God for ever and ever: for wisdom and might are his: And he changeth the times and the seasons: he removeth kings, and setteth up kings: he giveth wisdom unto the wise, and knowledge to them that know understanding: He revealeth the deep and secret things: he knoweth what *is* in the darkness, and the light dwelleth with him. (Dan 2:20-22 KJV)

Praise the Lord! Everything has a time, season and purpose. God reveals things as He desires, all wisdom and knowledge comes from Him. Daniel was shown the Kings dream with the interpretation and this saved him and his peers. There is Power when God reveals secrets. These devotions will bring revelation knowledge, understanding and transforming power to your life.

All numbers, names, dates, events have significance with the Lord Jesus. The number forty has a divine purpose.

This is why as instructed by the Holy Spirit I have compiled this forty day series.

We first see with Noah the rain fell for forty days and forty nights (see Gen 7). Moses encountered God on the Mount for forty days and forty nights (see Ex 24). Jesus was led by the Spirit to be tried of satan for forty days and forty nights (see Mat 4). Elijah journeyed on the strength of divine food for forty days and forty nights (see 1 Ki 19). Forty years the children of Israel wandered in the wilderness (see Det 2). At forty years old Moses slew the Egyptian and fled Egypt (see Act 7). Ezekiel prophesied that Egypt would be desolate forty years (Eze 29). All these and more important events match with the number forty.

The number forty can be seen as a time of testing, trial, judgment, transformation, testimony, victory, peace, promise, ending, new beginning and fulfillment. The Holy Spirit revealed to me that forty days is a time of intimacy, rest and transformation leading to the fulfillment of His purpose. Our obedience to His transforming instruction in forty days can result in our victory after forty days. Our disobedience to the Lords instruction can result in a delay of our full victory by forty years. Let us consider the scripture below;

You will die and your corpses will be scattered across this wilderness. Because you have complained against me, none of you over twenty years of age will enter that land. (Num 14:29 GNB)

You will suffer the consequences of your sin for forty years, one year for each of the forty days you spent

exploring the land. You will know what it means to have me against you! (Num 14:34 GNB)

Of all the spies who went to spy out the Promised Land only Joshua and Caleb gave a good report. The rest gave a bad report and complained they were also supported by the Israelites. As a result God said for every day spent spying the land, it shall be a year they shall spend wandering the desert. They also would not enter the Promised Land except for Joshua and Caleb. This was later fulfilled.

We can see the children of Israel were right at the doorstep of their promise after a forty day period they could have inherited their promise. Their disobedience and unbelief caused them to miss their promise and delay it's fulfillment by forty years!

Please understand this is not a formula that if you are disobedient your promise will be delayed by forty years but an example of a possibility.

Alternatively we see Jesus Christ who was led by the Holy Spirit soon after His public baptism into the desert for forty days and forty nights. He overcame the testing and temptation this led to the beginning of His ministry.

And there came a voice from heaven, *saying,* **Thou art my beloved Son, in whom I am well pleased. And immediately the Spirit driveth him into the wilderness. And he was there in the wilderness forty days, tempted of Satan; and was with the wild beasts; and the angels ministered unto him. Now after that John was put in prison, Jesus came into Galilee, preaching the gospel of the kingdom of God,** (Mar 1:11-14 KJV)

Here we see Jesus coming out from a forty day period to inherit His destiny as opposed to the disobedient children of Israel who delayed their destiny.

Let me emphasize that it does not take God forty days or forty years to fulfill His promises to you. This is not a fixed doctrine or formula for a breakthrough. Jesus Christ can do anything anytime. We must however acknowledge the significance and power forty days with the Lord has. As we have briefly seen many major events in the bible involved the number forty. This is not a law nor is it an Old Testament doctrine.

After his suffering, he showed himself to these men and gave many convincing proofs that he was alive. He appeared to them over a period of forty days and spoke about the kingdom of God. (Act 1:3 NIV)

Even in the New Testament as shown above forty days carries importance, for after Jesus rose from the dead He showed Himself for forty days before His ascension. These forty day devotions bring the life changing revelation of the specific topic by the Holy Ghost our teacher. Be blessed, encounter the Holy Spirit be transformed, rest, overcome and get your victory in Jesus name.

Jesus Christ the same yesterday, and to day, and for ever. (Heb 13:8 KJV)

LOVE EXPLAINED

Love is something that is the most misunderstood by people because it is who God is. The enemy has launched everything he can to distort the understanding of Love.

And unto man he said, Behold, the fear of the Lord, that *is* wisdom; and to depart from evil *is* understanding. (Job 28:28 KJV)

As you go through this book the Holy Spirit will bring understanding to you. As you receive understanding, evil will leave you. Every wrong idea you had of Love will be done away with. The media and mankind's corrupt culture has caused a great misrepresentation of love. We will bring the truth in this book.

Jesus told them another parable: "The kingdom of heaven is like a man who sowed good seed in his field. But while everyone was sleeping, his enemy came and sowed weeds among the wheat, and went away. (Mat 13:24-25 NIV)

It is not the fault of mankind that the picture of Love has been distorted. An enemy; the devil is the one who plants weeds after the good seed has been planted. Life is spiritual and must be understood first from the spirit. In the beginning God created paradise on earth all for Love of man whom He formed. He gave a simple instruction have dominion and do not eat from the tree of the knowledge of good and evil.

And the LORD God commanded the man, saying, Of every tree of the garden thou mayest freely eat: But of the tree of the knowledge of good and evil, thou shalt not eat of it: for in the day that thou eatest thereof thou shalt surely die. (Gen 2:16-17 KJV)

Then the enemy came immediately after the word was given. Only when the Lord brings the good seed; the truth, can the enemy come with a counterfeit lie. Love came first and then the opposite fear and torment came through the devil with his lies.

Now the serpent was more subtil than any beast of the field which the LORD God had made. And he said unto the woman, Yea, hath God said, Ye shall not eat of every tree of the garden?
(Gen 3:1 KJV)

The enemy came to question the truth. This is what he always does that is question the word of God. This creates uncertainty which brings fear and torment. Have you ever been unsure of a test result or waited for a financial or doctors report? When you're uncertain about the result it can be tormenting. Now what the enemy does is he becomes a commentator of all bad possibilities as you wait for the test results or report. On the other hand the Lord tells you firmly whatever the test or result says I am with you and will help you.

There is no fear in love; but perfect love casteth out fear: because fear hath torment. He that feareth is not made perfect in love. (1Jn 4:18 KJV)

Perfect Love which is the Love of God casts out fear and torment. Eve was tormented by the devil when she was being questioned and tempted. Throughout the Gospels we hear how people were tormented by evil spirits. Torment and temptation are evil based on fear and are totally against Love. So realise now that anything that brings fear and torment has absolutely nothing to do with Love.

Modern times have suggested that Love is a feeling, based on emotion that can change with circumstances. Or that their Love can be gained or lost. We hear the common saying "I don't love him/her anymore" in a relationship gone bad. Or that Love is based on blood relations. You may hear a mother saying "I love him he is my child". As well, we have those who Love based on friendship "I love my friend she has always been there for me". All these are not real Love but have been commonly spoken of as Love for ages.

True Love is the Love of God and that is what we will focus on in this book. Mankind has often mistaken the examples mentioned above wrongly as Love. We can just say they are a type of human love. Let's see the English definition of Love below.

Love is an intense, deep affection for another person. _Love_ also means to feel this intense affection for someone. _Love_ can also refer to a strong like for something or to like something a lot. _Love_ has many other senses both as a verb and a noun.

Re; Dictionary.com

Let's see the word Love as commonly translated in the King James Bible from the original Hebrew and Greek.

H157

אָהֵב   אָהַב

'âhab   'âhêb

aw-hab', aw-habe'

A primitive root; to *have affection* for (sexually or otherwise): - (be-) love (-d, -ly, -r), like, friend.

Re; Strong's Dictionary

The above Hebrew word is the most commonly translated as Love in the Old Testament. As you can see as in English it means affection. In the Greek there are two words often translated as Love.

G25

ἀγαπάω

agapaō

ag-ap-ah'-o

Perhaps from ἄγαν agan (*much*; or compare [H5689]); to *love* (in a social or moral sense): - (be-) love (-ed). Compare G5368.

G26

ἀγάπη

agapē

ag-ah'-pay

From G25; *love*, that is, *affection* or *benevolence*; specifically (plural) a *love feast:* - (feast of) charity ([-ably]), dear, love.

These two words Agapao and Agape are the most commonly translated as Love in the New Testament. Both mean affection and care with Agapao being a lighter Love and Agape a heavier Love. We will briefly speak on the lighter human forms of Love but our focus will be on Agape; the God kind of Love.

As I've studied the Word of God I came to realize by revelation from the Lord there are five types of Love.

1. Love for something

And make tasty meat for me, such as I love, and bring to me so that I may eat, that my soul may bless you before I die.
(Gen 27:4 MKJV)

2. Marital or sexual Love

And Jacob served seven years for Rachel, and they seemed to him a few days, for the love he had for her.
(Gen 29:20 MKJV)

3. Love for God

And shewing mercy unto thousands of them that love me, and keep my commandments.
(Exo 20:6 KJV)

4. Love for a Friend/Relative/Acquaintance

And if the servant shall plainly say, I love my master, my wife, and my children; I will not go out free:
(Exo 21:5 KJV)

5. God's Love

The LORD did not set his love upon you, nor choose you, because ye were more in number than any people; for ye *were* the fewest of all people:
(Deu 7:7 KJV)

Whenever we speak of Love it will resonate with one of the above five. There are also four types of Love commonly taught as expressed in the Greek language. Storge; the family kind of Love. Phileo; the friendship kind of Love. Eros; the sexual kind of Love. Agape; the God kind of Love. These are also good to know for better understanding. However the five types of Love is where everything circles around.

1. Love for something
2. Marital or sexual Love (Eros)
3. Love for God
4. Love for a friend, relative or acquaintance (Storge/Phileo)
5. God's Love (Agape)

Love functions in one of the five categories above. The bible clearly defines for us what Love is.

The one who does not love has not known God. For God is love. (1Jn 4:8 MKJV)

God is Love. This is the true definition of Love; God. So realize Love is not an emotion, not a feeling, not a desire but it is God. That means Love is a choice. God is a choice, people can choose to follow God or not. Get this right now whenever anyone speaks of Love it must have the attributes of God. Any expression or mention of Love without God is not Love, for God is Love itself.

We will delve deeper into Love and your spirit, soul and body will be impacted greatly. This will bring great freedom, peace and life in and around you.

Perfect Love which is the Love of God casts out fear and torment.

Get this right now whenever anyone speaks of Love it must have the attributes of God. Any expression or mention of Love without God is not Love, for God is Love itself.

God's Love, Natural Love & Wrong "love" – Day 1

Beloved, let us love one another: for love is of God; and every one that loveth is born of God, and knoweth God. He that loveth not knoweth not God; for God is love. (1Jn 4:7-8 KJV)

In our introduction to this book we revealed some core truths on Love. If you haven't yet read that make sure you do before reading here. God's Love is different from natural human love. Then we also have what we can call "wrong love" which is often called Love and spoken of as Love but is not Love at all.

Let's begin by understanding real Love, which is the Love of God that is God's Love.

But God commendeth his love toward us, in that, while we were yet sinners, Christ died for us. (Rom 5:8 KJV)

As we know Love is a strong affection and desire for someone or something. Now God had Love for us even when we were sinners, even when we did not have any care or concern for Him. That is real Love. This is Love which is independent of the actions of the receiver. In fact it is Love which is unchanged even though the one being loved is against their lover. This is what it means when God loved us while we were sinners. Can you imagine loving someone who is utterly against you?

The Love of God is unconditional. It does not depend on

anything and it does not change. Human Love on the other hand depends on a number of things. <u>Natural human Love</u> can be seen as the Love of a parent for their child.

And Isaac loved Esau, because he did eat of *his* **venison: but Rebekah loved Jacob.**
(Gen 25:28 KJV)

This is a natural kind of Love because it is based on the condition that this is someone from them, their blood; a part of them. This is an in built behavior God has given. This is why someone can be a murderer but Love their child. It is instinctive even animals naturally care for their children. This is not the Love of God. We see how Isaac loved his children but he loved Esau more because he loved his food. Rebekah loved her children but she loved Jacob more because he was a mommy's boy!

Natural human Love is also seen in friendships and relationships. When you've known someone from school or work you develop a relation with them. Although it's not blood but you will naturally, instinctively care for them more than a stranger because you know them. This is not the Love of God.

And it came to pass, when he had made an end of speaking unto Saul, that the soul of Jonathan was knit with the soul of David, and Jonathan loved him as his own soul. And Saul took him that day, and would let him go no more home to his father's house.
(1Sa 18:1-2 KJV)

Jonathan and David had a form of natural love through friendship. King Saul initially also had love for David because of what he did for him. Natural human Love is not the Love of God because it is based on conditions and can change. We see it clearly with Saul who loved David and lived with him who then turned to hunt David like a criminal.

David stayed in hiding in the hill country, in the wilderness near Ziph. Saul was always trying to find him, but God did not turn David over to him. David saw that Saul was out to kill him. David was at Horesh, in the wilderness near Ziph.
(1Sa 23:14-15 GNB)

This is human Love it is not genuine it has conditions. It works on a tit for tat basis. You scratch my back and I'll scratch yours. If there is a benefit in the relationship there is what they call "love" but it's not real. There is no real truth. God is Love so if it is real Love it must have the nature of God. Understand me, human Love is not wrong it is just normal and there is nothing amazing about it. Natural Love is expected. You'd expect someone to love a relative, a lifelong friend and so on. All this however is not the Love of God.

Probably the most misunderstood view of Love is in a sexual/marital relationship. Again this is natural Love which is given by God. It is not wrong for a man to have a sexual form of Love for a woman and vice versa. It is an in built trait God has given as a form of Love.

Jacob loved Rachel. So he offered, "I'll work seven years in return for your younger daughter Rachel."

Laban responded, "It's better that I give her to you than to any other man. Stay with me." Jacob worked seven years in return for Rachel, but the years seemed like only a few days to him because he loved her. At the end of the seven years Jacob said to Laban, "The time is up; give me my wife! I want to sleep with her."
(Gen 29:18-21 GW)

Jacob was attracted and so Loved Rachel that he worked seven years for her. This was a Godly kind of Love however it is motivated by the attractive desire. God's Love doesn't depend on looks or attractiveness. Eros kind of Love is what most people believe to be Love.

Perhaps you picked up this book because you wanted to understand Love as it is in a man and woman relationship. That is not wrong. However this is how the enemy has trapped people into thinking it's the only form of Love. The sexual erotic Love, why would you think this is? It's because this form of Love is focused around fulfilling desires. The devil then distorts what is right to be all about lust, manipulation, desire and pleasure.

The Lord actually designed the intimacy of Eros to be enjoyed in the Eros Love context. The enemy however sells the intimacy without the truth. As a result men use women for pleasure, women feel used and vice versa. This is the sin the Lord said is against your own body; sexual sin.

Avoid immorality. Any other sin a man commits does not affect his body; but the man who is guilty of sexual immorality sins against his own body.
(1Co 6:18 GNB)

Contrary to what some believe there are differences in sin. It is true that a sin no matter how small or big has the same effect which is separation from the Lord. Take note however there are some sins which are worse than others, the Word shows us this. Even Jesus mentioned when someone committed a greater sin that was Judas.

Jesus answered, "You could have no power at all against Me unless it had been given you from above. Therefore the one who delivered Me to you has the greater sin." (Joh 19:11 NKJV)

Sexual sin is destruction of your own body. Other sins are outside the body but this one is termed to be against your body which is also Christ's body. This is why the enemy so much pushes what he terms "love" under Eros but is actually lust. This is where we come to the third part in this day one heading that is wrong "love".

<u>Wrong "love"</u> is not Love at all. It is perversion. It is strong affection where it shouldn't be. It is driven by self pleasure. We see this in the bible with King David's son Amnon.

And he said to him, O son of the king, why are you getting thinner day by day? will you not say what your trouble is? And Amnon said to him, I am in love with Tamar, my brother Absalom's sister. (2Sa 13:4 BBE)

Amnon had what the English language can say is "love" for his sister. We call this "wrong love" that is affection which is wrong. He then planned to sleep with his sister Tamar. He raped her but soon after raping her and *fulfilling his desires he hated her.*

But he would not listen to her; and since he was stronger than she was, he overpowered her and raped her. Then Amnon was filled with a deep hatred for her; he hated her now even more than he had loved her before. He said to her, "Get out!" "No," she answered. "To send me away like this is a greater crime than what you just did!" But Amnon would not listen to her; he called in his personal servant and said, "Get this woman out of my sight! Throw her out and lock the door!" (2Sa 13:14-17 GNB)

The result of "wrong love" is wickedness. It is not Love it is perversion. It's sad that many young ladies fall prey to the "I love you" statement which is actually "I want you". That is what Amnon meant. Wrong love can even be seen in a possession. Where someone "loves" their car for an example so much they get furious if someone scratches it slightly and can even beat up someone. Love does not work ill towards his neighbour. If ever "love" causes you to sin its "wrong love". Love does not lead to sin.

Judas had "wrong love" for material things and sold Jesus. Solomon had "wrong love" for strange women and forsook the Lord. Saul had "wrong love" of pleasing people and lost his kingship. The religious leaders in Jesus' day had "wrong love" for people's honour and not honour from God.

Even then, many Jewish authorities believed in Jesus; but because of the Pharisees they did not talk about it openly, so as not to be expelled from the synagogue.

They loved human approval rather than the approval of God. (Joh 12:42-43 GNB)

The Love of God is real Love. Natural human Love has a form of God's Love but is not true Love. Wrong love is perverted affection and leads to sin. We all have natural Love but should aim for the God kind of Love; Agape.

Act

Eliminate "wrong love", keep your natural Love and grow to the God kind of Love.

Now God had Love for us even when we were sinners, even when we did not have any care or concern for Him. That is real Love. This is Love which is independent of the actions of the receiver. In fact it is Love which is unchanged even though the one being loved is against their lover. This is what it means when God loved us while we were sinners.

God Loved You First – Day 2

We love him, because he first loved us. (1Jn 4:19 KJV)

Those three little words; "I love you" have a powerful meaning when said with the backing of the heart. There is the casual way of saying it as among family and friends. When it comes for an example to the Eros kind of Love however, saying "I love you" for the first time is a big deal. Couples later on in years can even debate as to who said it first. This would be a claim that they loved the other first. This would appear to show the one who said it first as having the greater Love. That debate can go on endlessly as one may say "I loved you first I just didn't say it." As a couple that is not important as it is often driven by pride. The important thing is that you love each other. With the Lord however He has proof that He loved you first!

Herein is love, not that we loved God, but that he loved us, and sent his Son *to be* the propitiation for our sins. (1Jn 4:10 KJV)

Before we were even born God already loved us and knew us. We cannot say that we chose Jesus or by our wisdom came to Him. It is solely because of His great Love for us that we came to Him. God proved that He loved us by the crucifixion which was pre planned. The greatest sacrifice the death of His only son. Which in fact was God sacrificing Himself for you because He loved you.

Even before the world was made, God had already chosen us to be his through our union with Christ, so that we would be holy and without fault before him. Because of his love (Eph 1:4 GNB)

Predestination is the plan the Lord has set up for people in advance, that is His Will. Someone however has a choice to follow God's Will and not their own Will. At the same time there is the devil who's Will is simply to destroy God's Will for your life. That means God did not just Love you first so you can do what He desires for you. He knew that you could choose to reject His Love as some people have done. He still loves them eternally even though they rejected Him. His Love never changes.

"I call heaven and earth as witnesses today against you, that I have set before you life and death, blessing and cursing; therefore choose life, that both you and your descendants may live; "that you may love the LORD your God, that you may obey His voice, and that you may cling to Him, for He is your life and the length of your days; and that you may dwell in the land which the LORD swore to your fathers, to Abraham, Isaac, and Jacob, to give them." (Deu 30:19-20 NKJV)

Everyone should know that God loved them first. After that one must choose to accept His Love and enjoy life or reject His Love and suffer death. The Love of God removes all sin and brings about life. Absence of the Love of God brings about sin and death. This is the truth whether someone wants to hear or believe it or not. God has proposed His Love to you, do you accept? The beginning of acceptance is receiving Jesus as your Lord. This is the grace of God; His Love. This Love comes not because we deserve to be loved but just because God chose to Love us. No one can claim they deserve God's Love; it's all by favour that He loves us. We must embrace His Love.

Declaration

I declare that Jesus loved me first and I accept His love. Jesus is my Lord and my Saviour, I choose life. Amen

---

God proved that He loved us by the crucifixion which was pre planned. The greatest sacrifice the death of His only son. Which in fact was God sacrificing Himself for you because He loved you.

Mercy Triggers Love- Day 3

"Therefore I say to you, her sins, which are many, are forgiven, for she loved much. But to whom little is forgiven, the same loves little."
(Luk 7:47 NKJV)

The Gospel of Luke gives a wonderful account of a woman who was a well known sinner and Jesus. This lady gate crashed a dinner party and caused quite a stir. Many assume that she was a prostitute but that is not confirmed anywhere in scripture. What we do know is that she was a big time sinner.

One of the Pharisees asked Jesus to dine with him, and He went into the Pharisee's house and reclined at table. And behold, a woman of the town who was an especially wicked sinner, when she learned that He was reclining at table in the Pharisee's house, brought an alabaster flask of ointment (perfume). And standing behind Him at His feet weeping, she began to wet His feet with [her] tears; and she wiped them with the hair of her head and kissed His feet [affectionately] and anointed them with the ointment (perfume).
(Luk 7:36-38 AMP)

The actions of this uninvited guest caused the host to question whether Jesus was a prophet. The Pharisee Simon who was the host obviously knew this woman was bad news. This is why in his mind he thought Jesus ought to know this woman is wicked and should not let her touch him.

But seeing this, the Pharisee who had invited Him, spoke within himself, saying, This man, if he were a prophet, would have known who and what kind of woman this is who touches him, for she is a sinner.
(Luk 7:39 MKJV)

Jesus then knowing what Simon was thinking gave him an answer which shocked him. Take note, Simon did not speak this out loud neither did he ask a question. Jesus however spoke to Simon which confirmed Jesus knew that the woman was a big sinner and what Simon was thinking. What followed was a revelation of how God's mercy unleashed Love.

And Jesus answered and said to him, "Simon, I have something to say to you." So he said, "Teacher, say it." "There was a certain creditor who had two debtors. One owed five hundred denarii, and the other fifty. "And when they had nothing with which to repay, he freely forgave them both. Tell Me, therefore, which of them will love him more?" Simon answered and said, "I suppose the one whom he forgave more." And He said to him, "You have rightly judged."
(Luk 7:40-43 NKJV)

Jesus by revelation explained to Simon that the woman was ten times the sinner Simon was but was forgiven just as Simon was forgiven. Now Simon was the Host but did not do what was expected in that day to honour a guest. This showed the lower level of Love that Simon had for the master. This woman on the other hand broke all protocol and risked her life. As no one in particular a woman could just break in and interrupt a Pharisees dinner party. Neither could a woman approach a Rabbi as she did. It was also uncustomary for a woman to let her hair down in public. All these actions were wrong in the eyes of anyone who was at this dinner. In the eyes of Jesus however it was a sign of great Love in action because of His Mercy.

Then he turned to the woman and said to Simon, "Look at this woman kneeling here. When I entered your home, you didn't offer me water to wash the dust from my feet, but she has washed them with her tears and wiped them with her hair. You didn't give me a kiss of greeting, but she has kissed my feet again and again from the time I first came in. You neglected the courtesy of olive oil to anoint my head, but she has anointed my feet with rare perfume. I tell you, her sins – and they are many – have been forgiven, so she has shown me much love. But a person who is forgiven little shows only little love." **Then Jesus said to the woman,** "Your sins are forgiven."
(Luk 7:44-48 NLT-r)

Throughout the bible accounts like this reveal what great forgiveness does to a person. There is a higher level of Love when someone receives and realizes they have been accepted and forgiven. Simon had not experienced the power of the Mercy of God and therefore could not relate with the actions of the woman. The revelation Jesus gave him had to bring this to his attention. We see this with Saul who risked his life for the Lord Jesus. He was a partaker of the mercy of God which produced Love in him. Let's hear his words below.

And I thank Christ Jesus our Lord, who hath enabled

me, for that he counted me faithful, putting me into the ministry; Who was before a blasphemer, and a persecutor, and injurious: but I obtained mercy, because I did *it* ignorantly in unbelief. And the grace of our Lord was exceeding abundant with faith and love which is in Christ Jesus. This *is* a faithful saying, and worthy of all acceptation, that Christ Jesus came into the world to save sinners; of whom I am chief. Howbeit for this cause I obtained mercy, that in me first Jesus Christ might shew forth all longsuffering, for a pattern to them which should hereafter believe on him to life everlasting.

(1Ti 1:12-16 KJV)

God's Love is seen in His mercy. The Apostle Paul acknowledged that it was the Love of Christ Jesus that saved him. This is why in life you will continually hear testimonies of people who are extremely radical for Jesus who were once the worst of sinners. The Lord is good and His mercy endures forever. To know His mercy is to know Him.

For more on Mercy read Forty Days On Mercy by Jason Pullen

Act

Learn to be merciful like Jesus and trigger Love.

There is a higher level of Love when someone receives and realizes they have been accepted and forgiven.

Love Yourself – Day 4

If ye fulfil the royal law according to the scripture, Thou shalt love thy neighbour as thyself, ye do well:
(Jas 2:8 KJV)

To Love your neighbour as yourself is one of the most taught things in churches. However I'm certain that not everyone truly understands this. Many mistakenly think it means Love your neighbour first. It actually means Love yourself first and then Love your neighbour. Others may interpret this as being selfish. It is not being selfish in fact it is what Jesus taught!

And Jesus answered him, The first of all the commandments *is,* Hear, O Israel; The Lord our God is one Lord: And thou shalt love the Lord thy God with all thy heart, and with all thy soul, and with all thy mind, and with all thy strength: this *is* the first commandment. And the second *is* like, *namely* this, Thou shalt love thy neighbour as thyself. There is none other commandment greater than these.
(Mar 12:29-31 KJV)

Jesus was asked which the first commandment is but in His answer Jesus mentioned the second commandment as well. Why did He do this? He did this because the first commandment is fully attached to the second. First Love God with your all and second Love your neighbour as yourself. God first then yourself then treat your neighbour like yourself.

Many Christians do not Love themselves. Wrong teaching has caused them to think that self Love is arrogance, pride and selfishness. Self Love is what will cause someone to know how to Love someone else. Know how to treat and value yourself first then you will know how to treat and value others.

"Therefore, whatever you want men to do to you, do also to them, for this is the Law and the Prophets. (Mat 7:12 NKJV)

You can decide how to treat yourself and how others treat you; this is a measure of self Love. The way you treat your Spirit, soul and body reflects your level of self Love. If you feed your Spirit the Word of God you Love yourself. If you allow your soul to hear, see and feel righteousness you Love yourself. If you look after your body, exercise and do not over eat or engage in substances that will destroy your body you Love yourself. The opposite of these actions would mean you do not Love yourself.

When someone loves themselves they have a sense of value, respect, confidence, high self esteem, significance and influence. When someone does not truly Love themselves they do not know their value, worth, have low self esteem, low self confidence, feel irrelevant with little significance and influence. This is how you can measure your self-Love.

If you do not Love yourself you will not know how to Love your neighbour. Jesus never undermined Himself, spoke badly about Himself or had low self esteem or lacked significance and influence. Jesus loved Himself. Listen to how Jesus spoke about Himself.

As long as I am in the world, I am the light of the world. (Joh 9:5 KJV) I am the door: by me if any man enter in, he shall be saved, and shall go in and out, and find pasture. (Joh 10:9 KJV) I am the good shepherd: the good shepherd giveth his life for the sheep. (Joh 10:11 KJV) I am the true vine, and my Father is the husbandman. (Joh 15:1 KJV)

Jesus used "I" a lot, it is often taught that when a person continually uses "I" they are proud. This is where one needs to understand that there is a difference between self pride and pride in general. A world class painter can have self pride in his work and will not accept any negative comment. To the world class painter his painting is valuable and anyone who doesn't value it doesn't understand his work. This is different to a bad painter who talks up his painting, never takes any criticism and yet never produces anything valuable. That is pride.

Jesus was accused of pride and arrogance. Yet Jesus just knew where He came from, who He was and what He was worth. It is not pride to speak well of yourself. You must Love yourself. Many people had their own perception of Jesus but He was not moved by that. Jesus knew His father knew Him and loved Him and that's what mattered to Him.

We ought to follow the footsteps of Jesus. People will always have something to say about you good and bad. What they say about you is irrelevant. You know yourself more than anyone besides God. Never be moved by peoples praise or criticism. John the Baptist knew who he was and spoke like Jesus.

He said, I *am* the voice of one crying in the wilderness, Make straight the way of the Lord, as said the prophet Esaias. (Joh 1:23 KJV)

The Apostle John knew who he was and loved himself that is why he is even known as John the beloved.

Then Peter, turning about, seeth the disciple whom Jesus loved following; which also leaned on his breast at supper, and said, Lord, which is he that betrayeth thee? (Joh 21:20 KJV)

Moses when writing about himself (under the inspiration of the Holy Ghost of course) referred to himself as the most humble person in the world.

(Now Moses was a very humble man, more humble than anyone else on the face of the earth.)
(Num 12:3 NIV)

The Apostle Paul boldly declared that the Gospel he preached was from God alone and no man taught him.

But I make known to you, brethren, that the gospel which was preached by me is not according to man. For I neither received it from man, nor was I taught it, but it came through the revelation of Jesus Christ.
(Gal 1:11-12 NKJV)

Anyone without the Spirit of God or who is a baby Christian can think that whoever speaks like the above examples is proud and arrogant. No, a thousand times no! When you know who you are and your worth you will value yourself and Love yourself. For instance when Moses wrote that he was the most humble it's the same time that the Lord called out Aaron and Miriam for speaking against Moses. Ask the Lord who you truly are and never walk around as though you have to apologize for your existence.

For you know that it was not with perishable things such as silver or gold that you were redeemed from the empty way of life handed down to you from your forefathers, (1Pe 1:18 NIV)

Never accept someone other than your heavenly father to tell you your worth! It cost God nothing to create the entire heaven and earth. But it cost God His very life to buy you back. That is your value. The entire universe could not pay for your salvation. This is your value as a born again believer.

What this means is that those who become Christians become new persons. They are not the same anymore, for the old life is gone. A new life has begun! All this newness of life is from God, who brought us back to himself through what Christ did. And God has given us the task of reconciling people to him.
(2Co 5:17-18 NLT)

When you have a very precious item you lock it up and treasure it. This is why businesses have strong rooms to lock away valuables. Again in the strong room there are safes to lock away the even more valuable things. As a woman or a man too, how you carry yourself and dress shows how much you value and Love yourself. Anything which is cheap is seen everywhere and handled by everyone. Value your body and Love yourself.

Do you not know that you are the temple of God and that the Spirit of God dwells in you? If anyone defiles the temple of God, God will destroy him. For the temple of God is holy, which temple you are.
(1Co 3:16-17 NKJV)

When you learn your value which is what I am teaching you now, you will Love yourself more. This will in turn enable you to Love your neighbour as yourself. You are not a door mat! If you have experienced an abusive relationship where you were insulted and called valueless. Or perhaps you are experiencing that relationship now.
(Ask the Lord to help you get out of that abuse, the person change or you get out)

I am here to tell you that as a born again child of God you are valuable! What your ex-partner, parent, teacher, boss or any other thinks of your value is not your value. Abusive relationships are a tool of the devil used to stop someone from knowing who they are and unleashing their true value to the world.

The Lord has revealed to me who I am and the value I have for this world. He sternly told me one of the ways I will see this is by how people receive me. This has been confirmed to me clearly as I have seen God lift people tremendously who have blessed me and seen terrible things happen to those who trouble me. He has assured me at times when I pray for Him to uplift those who bless me that He will even if I didn't pray. At times when I pray for mercy upon those who trouble me He says "step aside Jason it is a righteous thing for me to recompense tribulation for those who trouble you".

Know your value child of God treat yourself well. Do not accept wrong treatment in the name of Love or humility. At the same time don't try and prove anything God will. Jesus did not accept any kind of treatment, He knew His worth. He rode on a brand new donkey, similar to riding in a brand new car. He did not reject the praises of the people at His triumphal entry.

Go to the village ahead of you, and as you enter it, you will find a colt tied there, which no one has ever ridden. Untie it and bring it here. (Luk 19:30 NIV)

Saying, Blessed *be* the King that cometh in the name of the Lord: peace in heaven, and glory in the highest. And some of the Pharisees from among the multitude said unto him, Master, rebuke thy disciples. And he answered and said unto them, I tell you that, if these should hold their peace, the stones would immediately cry out. (Luk 19:38-40 KJV)

A woman poured ointment on Him worth a full year's wages. His disciples saw it as a waste but Jesus saw it as honour for His worth. This was not arrogance or pride but Jesus knowing His value.

A woman came to Him having an alabaster flask of very costly fragrant oil, and she poured it on His head as He sat at the table. But when His disciples saw it, they were indignant, saying, "Why this waste? "For this fragrant oil might have been sold for much and given to the poor." But when Jesus was aware of it, He said to them, "Why do you trouble the woman? For she has done a good work for Me. "For you have the poor with you always, but Me you do not have always. (Mat 26:7-11 NKJV)

Jesus showed His value by explaining the value of His presence. Time is also a measure value. Work is often paid depending on the hours put in. Don't give time to people who don't value you. Give time to yourself. Not just in terms of luxury but more importantly time to invest and perfect the gifts God has put in you. Learn to forgive yourself and motivate yourself. Be good to yourself you are God's gift to the world. If you do not pursue and build your calling you will always help someone else pursue and build their calling.

To bury your gifts and calling is to hate and bury you. Give yourself as a blessing to the world. Love yourself, pursue your calling. Study the life of Jesus and see there is a balance in all we've spoken about. Love God, love yourself and love your neighbour. Do this with balance given by the Lord.

Declaration

I declare that I am born of God Therefore I am priceless and extremely precious. It cost the blood of Jesus to buy me back. I am worth the blood of Jesus. I declare that what God says about me is what matters. I will not be moved by what people say or think about me whether it is good or bad. God loves me and I love God. I declare that I will Love myself so that I will know how to Love my neighbour in Jesus name. Amen

If you do not Love yourself you will not know how to Love your neighbour. Jesus never undermined Himself, spoke badly about Himself or had low self esteem or lacked significance and influence. Jesus loved Himself.

To bury your gifts and calling is to hate and bury you.

Love Fulfills The Law – Day 5

For this, Thou shalt not commit adultery, Thou shalt not kill, Thou shalt not steal, Thou shalt not bear false witness, Thou shalt not covet; and if *there be* any other commandment, it is briefly comprehended in this saying, namely, Thou shalt love thy neighbour as thyself. Love worketh no ill to his neighbour: therefore love *is* the fulfilling of the law.
(Rom 13:9-10 KJV)

The Law of Moses was a heavy load which the Israelites failed to carry. Even Moses the giver of the law broke the law. All those "thou shalt nots" aimed to do one thing; to direct Israel to Love. The law could not be kept by man, only Jesus managed to keep the law and fulfill it. Jesus summed up all the many instructions the law gave, in a simple yet powerful way.

Master, which *is* the great commandment in the law? Jesus said unto him, Thou shalt love the Lord thy God with all thy heart, and with all thy soul, and with all thy mind. This is the first and great commandment. And the second *is* like unto it, Thou shalt love thy neighbour as thyself. On these two commandments hang all the law and the prophets.
(Mat 22:36-40 KJV)

By loving God and your neighbour as yourself you obey all the instructions, commandments and statutes of the law. The purpose of the law was to teach the "children" of Israel until Christ came. It was a shadow of the real image, the real thing which was Love in Christ. All the laws of keeping the Sabbath and so forth were made for "children" who needed a list of do's and don'ts. Mature sons of God understand that Love is what the law pointed to.

We are conscious that the law is good, if a man makes a right use of it, With the knowledge that the law is made, not for the upright man, but for those who have no respect for law and order, for evil men and sinners, for the unholy and those who have no religion, for those who put their fathers or mothers to death, for takers of life, For those who go after loose women, for those with unnatural desires, for those who take men prisoners, who make false statements and false oaths, and those who do any other things against the right teaching, (1Ti 1:8-10 BBE)

The law was made to identify a law breaker and show them what they were doing was wrong. It can still be used as Jesus did in His ministry to show the Pharisees they were guilty too when they wanted to stone the woman caught in adultery. It is used only to show a sinner their error. Children and the disobedient need laws to show them they've misbehaved. A mature and obedient son is simply told what grace and truth says, that is Love God and your neighbour as yourself. By doing this you are fulfilling the law.

Love worketh no ill to his neighbour: therefore love *is* the fulfilling of the law.
(Rom 13:10 KJV)

Love will never do anything bad towards its neighbour. If you Love your neighbour you won't plan evil against them. If you Love your neighbour you won't gossip about them. If you Love your neighbour you will forgive them and talk to them. If you Love your neighbour your hearts intention will always be to bless them, help them and never harm them. Even under the law the children of Israel were commanded to Love strangers!

"Do not exploit the foreigners who live in your land. They should be treated like everyone else, and you must love them as you love yourself. Remember that you were once foreigners in the land of Egypt. I, the LORD, am your God.
(Lev 19:33-34 NLT)

Do you want to know if you are living a righteous life as God requires of you? Then just practice Love without conditions and without partiality. That means if someone wrongs you forgive them because forgiveness is Love. You cannot say you have forgiven and you get angry or bitter when you think of someone. That is not Love. Even if you believe they were wrong or everyone knows they were wrong. Love forgives and forgets! It is evil to only Love those you feel are deserving of your Love. We must Love especially those you see as your enemies.

If ye fulfil the royal law according to the scripture, Thou shalt love thy neighbour as thyself, ye do well: But if ye have respect to persons, ye commit sin, and are convinced of the law as transgressors.
(Jas 2:8-9 KJV)

In life I have ministered to people who have committed terrible acts like murder for an example. These people have given their life to Christ and the main thing all of them ask for as a prayer request is for the family of the people they killed to forgive them. They ask for this with bleeding hearts and tears. They know God has forgiven them but seek the one they wronged to forgive them. Those who have managed to reconcile and were forgiven feel genuine Love. Withholding Love is also to withhold forgiveness.

"If you forgive those who sin against you, your heavenly Father will forgive you. But if you refuse to forgive others, your Father will not forgive your sins. (Mat 6:14-15 NLT-r)

Love fulfills the law. Jesus compared anger to murder and adultery to a lustful imagination. He was pointing it as sin not just the resulting action of anger and lust as sin. Unforgiveness is equally not Love and is a breaking of the law which also means you won't be forgiven.

Remember whatever you would want done to you do it to all. Be truthful and not subjective and you will be blessed. Even if it's your adulterous ex marital partner forgive them, abusive person from your past, cruel leader and so on. Forgive and pray for them to be blessed not cursed. Don't keep speaking of the evil they did to you! This confirms Love.

For if ye love them which love you, what reward have ye? do not even the publicans the same? And if ye salute your brethren only, what do ye more *than others?* do not even the publicans so? Be ye therefore

perfect, even as your Father which is in heaven is perfect. (Mat 5:46-48 KJV)

As you welcome the Word of God into your heart you will be changed and will have the ability to Love just like Jesus. A natural carnal person cannot do this. A child of God is born of Love and it is their nature to Love. Do not fight your nature and allow the enemy to work evil through you. Let Love lead you.

Declaration

I declare that I am born of God. I have the nature of Jesus in me. I have the natural spiritual ability to Love my neighbour as myself. I fulfill the law through Love. And I know that Love does not work ill or evil in Jesus name. Amen

---

Do you want to know if you are living a righteous life as God requires of you? Then just practice Love without conditions and without partiality.

The Love Of God In Your Heart – Day 6

And hope maketh not ashamed; because the love of God is shed abroad in our hearts by the Holy Ghost which is given unto us. (Rom 5:5 KJV)

Hope is an anchor and a divine connection to great expectations of the future. We have faith that our future is brighter because of hope. The only way in which we can be sure of this is because God's Love has been divinely put in our hearts. It is this gift of faith given to born again believers. You know, that you know, that you know, that Jesus loves you and died for you. God has printed this on your heart.

"I will give you a new heart and put a new spirit within you; I will take the heart of stone out of your flesh and give you a heart of flesh. "I will put My Spirit within you and cause you to walk in My statutes, and you will keep My judgments and do them. (Eze 36:26-27 NKJV)

The Israelites who the Lord made a covenant with through Moses were hard hearted and stiff necked. This means they were insensitive and stubborn. The Lord promised to remove the heart of stone with a soft heart of flesh. A heart of flesh means a heart sensitive to the Spirit of God. In the New Testament God has not written His laws on tables of stone as He previously did through Moses. He has written them on our hearts!

"For this is the covenant that I will make with the

house of Israel after those days, says the LORD: I will put My laws in their mind and write them on their hearts; and I will be their God, and they shall be My people. "None of them shall teach his neighbor, and none his brother, saying, 'Know the LORD,' for all shall know Me, from the least of them to the greatest of them. (Heb 8:10-11 NKJV)

The law of God is the mind of God. Any loving parent gives instructions to their children to benefit them. I'm certain if it were possible to imprint these instructions in the minds and hearts of their children they'd do it! This is what God has done. He has printed His Word which is His love in the hearts of His children. Even the Apostle Paul brought this revelation that our hearts receive the Word of God as an imprint by the Holy Spirit.

Ye are our epistle written in our hearts, known and read of all men: *Forasmuch as ye are* **manifestly declared to be the epistle of Christ ministered by us, written not with ink, but with the Spirit of the living God; not in tables of stone, but in fleshy tables of the heart.** (2Co 3:2-3 KJV)

What as a Christian you may have thought was your conscience is actually the Love of God shed in your heart. By the blood of Jesus Christ it has been made possible. No longer do you need to look outward at a stone carved with instructions but look within yourself. You are born again and born of Love. Jesus said whatever comes from the heart is what truly matters. Anyone who is not born of God does not have the Love of God in their heart. That means they are not a child of God but a child of the devil.

But you are not living the life of the flesh, you are living the life of the Spirit, if the [Holy] Spirit of God [really] dwells within you [directs and controls you]. But if anyone does not possess the [Holy] Spirit of Christ, he is none of His [he does not belong to Christ, is not truly a child of God]. [Rom. 8:14.] (Rom 8:9 AMP)

And He said, "What comes out of a man, that defiles a man. "For from within, out of the heart of men, proceed evil thoughts, adulteries, fornications, murders, "thefts, covetousness, wickedness, deceit, lewdness, an evil eye, blasphemy, pride, foolishness. "All these evil things come from within and defile a man." (Mar 7:20-23 NKJV)

An unsaved person is not a child of God therefore God's Love is not in them. Every form of evil comes from such people because they are not yet born of Love. As a Christian born of Love, God's Love is in your heart. His Word in your heart is what makes it possible for you to do good. This is why I often say a child of God has to consciously fight their nature to do evil because evil is not in them. Love is in you as a child of God, therefore choose Love.

Confession

I confess that the Love of God has been shed abroad in my heart. This Love leads me guides me and causes me to do good in life. The Word of God is printed on my heart in Jesus name. Amen

Any loving parent gives instructions to their children to benefit them. I'm certain if it were possible to imprint these instructions in the minds and hearts of their children they'd do it! This is what God has done. He has printed His Word which is His love in the hearts of His children.

A New Commandment – Day 7

A new commandment I give unto you, That ye love one another; as I have loved you, that ye also love one another. (Joh 13:34 KJV)

In the Old Testament the Lord made a covenant with the Israelites which had a foundation of Ten Commandments. When Jesus came and ministered to the Israelites He made it clear that He did not go against the law and Moses but fulfilled the Law of Moses. This included the Ten Commandments.

"Do not think that I came to destroy the Law or the Prophets. I did not come to destroy but to fulfill. "For assuredly, I say to you, till heaven and earth pass away, one jot or one tittle will by no means pass from the law till all is fulfilled. "Whoever therefore breaks one of the least of these commandments, and teaches men so, shall be called least in the kingdom of heaven; but whoever does and teaches them, he shall be called great in the kingdom of heaven. (Mat 5:17-19 NKJV)

Jesus fulfilled the law for us by living a sinless life which we could not do. He still emphasized the importance of the law. The first of the Ten Commandments is to have no other gods but Him, the second is not to make any image or god and worship it. The third is to not use the Lord's name in vain. All these commandments except number four to keep the Sabbath and number five honour your father and mother were instructions what not to do.

When entering the Promised Land however Moses was given other commandments, statutes and judgments to teach the children of Israel. The first of those instructions which was for the benefit of the Israelites was to Love God. This was an instruction on what they should do, not what they should not do.

"Hear, O Israel: The LORD our God, the LORD is one! "You shall love the LORD your God with all your heart, with all your soul, and with all your strength. "And these words which I command you today shall be in your heart. (Deu 6:4-6 NKJV)

The instructions that followed had reasons to them. The Lord was now relating differently than He did previously. With the Ten Commandments it was more of don't do this. Now He was saying you are going into your inheritance, the Promised Land so do this. This was more intimate. The law we know is made for a criminal not a righteous man. God was now preparing for those people who will enter the Promised Land. Jesus then came and said He is giving "A New Commandment" to His disciples.

"A new commandment I give to you, that you love one another; as I have loved you, that you also love one another. (Joh 13:34 NKJV)

This was "A New Commandment" because they had experienced Agape Love one on one in the flesh with Jesus. It was different to God saying Love me and Love your neighbour. They had God with them in the flesh (Jesus) who had shown them Love. This is when He said to His disciples as you have seen my example of Love so do likewise to each other.

Have you experienced the Grace, Mercy and Love of God in your life? The New Commandment is to Love as God has loved you. So when someone wrongs you remember how the Lord by Love forgave you and do the same. When someone is in need of compassion and care, remember how the Lord by His Love lifted you up and do the same. God loved you while you were a sinner so you should also Love people who are sinners knowing they can be saved by the Love of God working in you.

Confession

I confess that as I have been a partaker of the Love of Jesus Christ in my life I will also be a demonstrator of His Love in Jesus name. Amen

---

They had God with them in the flesh (Jesus) who had shown them Love. This is when He said to His disciples as you have seen my example of Love so do likewise to each other.

Love Covers A Multitude Of sins ~ Day 8

And above all things have fervent love for one another, for "love will cover a multitude of sins."
(1Pe 4:8 NKJV)

Have you ever had to cover up for someone? Maybe when you were younger one of your friends or siblings did something wrong and you had the opportunity to expose or hide their wrong doing. If this was your good friend you would probably do your best to hide what they did. In God's eyes this is Love in action. More specifically when the wrong done is against you. Say for an example you reported a theft of your property and then discovered who the thief was. In this case by not exposing the thief publicly and dropping the case you covered a multitude of sins. You could then approach the thief with the message of Salvation.

Brethren, if anyone among you wanders from the truth, and someone turns him back, let him know that he who turns a sinner from the error of his way will save a soul from death and cover a multitude of sins.
(Jas 5:19-20 NKJV)

To exercise mercy is an act of Love not wickedness. It is wicked to cover criminal actions PLEASE UNDERSTAND THE DIFFERENCE. It is when it is in your power to cover sins that you must forgive and forget. I'll share with you a personal experience. At one point in time the Holy Ghost revealed to me a plan a person had plotted against another person I knew. They put the plan into action as God had foretold me. Later I became aware of it. Instead of addressing this individual publicly, I approached them privately and rebuked them for what they were doing. I had several opportunities to expose with facts and evidence the plan of this person but I did not. Eventually their plan failed but I was not a contributor of their downfall. Love covers errors but still corrects. It gives an individual an opportunity to repent.

He that covereth a transgression seeketh love; but he that repeateth a matter separateth *very* friends. A reproof entereth more into a wise man than an hundred stripes into a fool.
(Pro 17:9-10 KJV)

Jesus dealt with sinners knowing all their wicked deeds. He did not however broadcast all their sins instead He showed them their error and gave them space to repent. To repent is to change your way of thinking and acting. We see this with Noah, Abraham, Moses, Rahab, David, Zacchaeus, Peter, Paul and many more. The Lord never amplified their wrong doing but their repentant actions. Not many people know of the errors of these heroes of faith but many know of their testimonies of victory. When Jesus died on the cross He covered all sins and gave an opportunity for all to change their ways.

In the Old Testament sacrifices had to be offered continually to cover sins for a season.

If they could have provided perfect cleansing, the sacrifices would have stopped, for the worshipers would have been purified once for all time, and their feelings of guilt would have disappeared. But just the

opposite happened. Those yearly sacrifices reminded them of their sins year after year. For it is not possible for the blood of bulls and goats to take away sins. (Heb 10:2-4 NLT)

The blood of Jesus on the other hand does not just cover sins but washes them away. What does this mean? It means the record of wrong doing does not exist with God! Love deletes the record of sins, there are no ex-convicts with God ex-sinners there are new creations. When your cover someone's wrong against you delete the record.

You will be merciful to us once again. You will trample our sins underfoot and send them to the bottom of the sea! (Mic 7:19 GNB)

And their sins and iniquities will I remember no more. Now where remission of these *is, there is* **no more offering for sin.** (Heb 10:17-18 KJV)

People were astonished by the ministry of Jesus. They would catch someone in the act of sin and demand judgment but Jesus would cause even the accusers to back off from their accusation.

The devil seeks to expose and point out sin and errors. If you ever find yourself as the one to publish someone's sins or faults even if they truly sinned and were wrong. Just know that you are an agent of the devil. Never allow yourself to be used by the kingdom of darkness.

Hell always wants sin to be known and published. It desires to bring down people in particular ministers of

God. If you find yourself in the crowd quoting a person's mistakes just know you are just like the hard hearted religious leaders in Jesus' day who desired to see sinners stoned to death.

So when they continued asking him, he lifted up himself, and said unto them, He that is without sin among you, let him first cast a stone at her.
(Joh 8:7 KJV)

Who are you to judge another's servant? To his own master he stands or falls. Indeed, he will be made to stand, for God is able to make him stand.
(Rom 14:4 NKJV)

You may want to see justice so does everyone; you may say there must be justice for those who suffer because of sinners. Remember the Lord is the judge and the judgment of Love is mercy! Those who will accept His mercy have their sins covered those who reject will fall. God is the judge.

Saul for instance was nothing short of a modern day terrorist against Christianity. Yet in all this Ananias and the early Church did not once pray for Saul to die.

Then Ananias answered, Lord, I have heard by many of this man, how much evil he hath done to thy saints at Jerusalem: And here he hath authority from the chief priests to bind all that call on thy name. But the Lord said unto him, Go thy way: for he is a chosen vessel unto me, to bear my name before the Gentiles, and kings, and the children of Israel: For I will shew him how great things he must suffer for my name's sake. And Ananias went his way, and entered into the house; and putting his hands on him said, Brother Saul, the Lord, *even* Jesus, that appeared unto thee in the way as thou camest, hath sent me, that thou mightest receive thy sight, and be filled with the Holy Ghost. (Act 9:13-17 KJV)

Ananias received an instruction to minister to Saul and in an instant did not see him as a murderer but as a brother. There could have been some Christians Ananias knew personally who died because of Saul. He did not say Lord avenge their blood. No he said, Brother Saul receive your sight! This is what Love does. Love cries out for forgiveness and mercy.

Act

As much as it is in your power to show mercy and cover sins do so. Give people an opportunity to repent. God is the judge.

Jesus dealt with sinners knowing all their wicked deeds. He did not however broadcast all their sins instead He showed them their error and gave them space to repent.

From death To Life Because Of Love – Day 9

We know that we have passed from death unto life, because we love the brethren. He that loveth not *his* brother abideth in death. (1Jn 3:14 KJV)

Life is easily understood by antonyms. The Gospel gives better understanding of life and has many antonyms too. These opposites stem from opposing forces of God and the devil. We have God on one side with every one of His characteristics and the devil on the other side with his characteristics. At the same time we obviously have God with His fruit and on the other hand the devil with his fruit. Each quality brings about a distinct result. Light and Love produces life whereas darkness and fear brings forth death. There is no middle ground everything is either of God or not; no wonder Jesus said whoever is not with Him is against Him!

He that is not with me is against me; and he that gathereth not with me scattereth abroad. (Mat 12:30 KJV)

The Word of God reveals that there is a transition from death to life by Love for the brethren. The Love that a child of God has for his fellow brothers and sisters in Christ transports them from the realm of death to the realm of life. This is God's side, the side where there is Love, light and life! Do you Love the family of God; born again believers? If you do then you have eternal life in you.

Whoever hates his brother is a murderer, and you know that no murderer has eternal life abiding in him. (1Jn 3:15 NKJV)

Have you ever seen a born again believer who hates a fellow born again believer? I have and this is clearly seen in the attitude some "christians" have towards other Christians. Not greeting or speaking to someone. We hear famous preachers who openly mock fellow preachers. This is sad but is a clear sign that these "christians" have hate towards their brother or sister in Christ. They kill and stone with words and actions.

This is the word translated as hate in the original text explained below.

G3404

μισέω

miseō

mis-eh'-o

From a primary word μῖσος misos (*hatred*); to *detest* (especially to *persecute*); by extension to *love less:* - hate (-ful).

Re; Strong's Dictionary

To hate, also meaning to detest, persecute and to love less. When someone can smile at every Christian but their face changes when they see another Christian, that's a sign of hate. To buy good gifts for everyone but a cheap gift, for say your mother in-law or daughter in-law is a sign of hate.

There is something that happens to an individual when they have encounters with the Lord Jesus Christ. Their capacity and ability to Love is enlarged. It is raised to levels people cannot even understand. For an example you are sacrificing to help a person or a group of people. Then they attack you by speaking badly about you behind your back. They may even confront you publicly as being a wicked person. In such an instance it seems sane to just walk away and stop all the good you are doing. If you were genuinely helping out of Love whatever anyone sys against you will not change what you were doing. In fact it can even give you more fire to do more.

This has happened to me several times in life. Each time it may be just a few bad apples that the devil uses to try and stop me from helping many. The easy thing would be to say; why am I even wasting my time and effort taking this evil as a reward. Then stop your labour of Love. By doing that the enemy prevails because there are other innocent souls who may suffer.

The Love that you have for the brethren, the people of God is what will enable you to keep running. You will not be moved by hate, you will overcome it with Love. I've witnessed projects being killed just because a few greedy people offended a donor. If the donor had Agape Love in them they would see how to remove the devils and keep going.

For in Christ Jesus neither circumcision nor uncircumcision avails anything, but faith working

through love. You ran well. Who hindered you from obeying the truth? This persuasion does not come **from Him who calls you.** (Gal 5:6-8 NKJV)

As a Christian we are born of a Love God. We are children of Love. The enemy is aware of this and will always try to either use you to stop someone from walking in Love (like the examples given above). Or the enemy will cause you to be offended and stir up hate in your heart for whatever reason. Whether you think you were right or wrong in a scenario, anything that causes you to hate must be removed! Hate produces murderers and murderers kill.

Whoever hates his brother is a murderer, and you know that no murderer has eternal life abiding in him. (1Jn 3:15 NKJV)

That little act of avoiding a person at all costs, always speaking badly about someone or only remembering the bad they did is hate. As a child of God you must resist the poison of hate at all costs. If not it will become a root of bitterness. God has nothing to do with bitterness and this will affect the life of God in you.

When someone is born again they receive eternal life into their Spirit but if they allow a root of bitterness evil can result. Jesus clearly said hate deserves judgment just like murder. Why did He say this? He did because it is the heart that matters. Just because you did not actually kill someone does not mean you did not kill them.

"You have heard that the law of Moses says, 'Do not murder. If you commit murder, you are subject to

judgment.' But I say, if you are angry with someone, you are subject to judgment! If you call someone an idiot, you are in danger of being brought before the high council. And if you curse someone, you are in danger of the fires of hell. "So if you are standing before the altar in the Temple, offering a sacrifice to God, and you suddenly remember that someone has something against you, leave your sacrifice there beside the altar. Go and be reconciled to that person. Then come and offer your sacrifice to God.
(Mat 5:21-24 NLT-r)

Pursue peace with all people, and holiness, without which no one will see the Lord: looking carefully lest anyone fall short of the grace of God; lest any root of bitterness springing up cause trouble, and by this many become defiled; (Heb 12:14-15 NKJV)

In this world you are bound to come across people who may offend you or who you just don't get along with. Now the Word of God says Love your fellow Christians and you move from death to life. It's a sign that God's eternal life is at work in you. That is different to saying Love the world (sinners) which we are also expected to do by the way.

"Love the brethren" doesn't mean you have to get along with everyone in Church or let everyone tramp on your toes and offend you and you do nothing about it. No! It means you never let hate work in you. By the word of God this is possible by Love. My experience which is confirmed by the Word of God is; do it so it can be done to you! We reap what we sow; forgive to be forgiven, Love to be loved.

An intimate relationship with Jesus gets you to see the weightier matters of life. You grow in Christ and are not moved by baby Christians or the devil using people to try and stop you from running your race. Your heart will be driven by the power of eternal life in you. This will change those hard hearted people. Jesus had so many reasons to forsake His assignment but He didn't. He gave us a new commandment to Love one another as He had loved. That was a message to the disciples! Jesus was emphasizing Love for our brothers and sisters in Christ. It's different to loving the world; He said first start by loving each other. That is brotherly kindness before charity. The world will be saved when they see the Love Christians have between one another.

And to godliness brotherly kindness; and to brotherly kindness charity.
(2Pe 1:7 KJV)

By this shall all *men* know that ye are my disciples, if ye have love one to another.
(Joh 13:35 KJV)

Prayer

Lord thank you for eternal life abiding in me. Let your Spirit continually work in me and through me. Let your Love in me be seen in my Love first for my fellow Christians. I rebuke any form of hate or bitterness that tries to rest in me. Keep me from ever being used by the enemy in Jesus name. Amen

There is something that happens to an individual when they have encounters with the Lord Jesus Christ. Their capacity and ability to Love is enlarged. It is raised to levels people cannot even understand.

To Love Is To Know God – Day 10

Beloved, let us love one another: for love is of God; and every one that loveth is born of God, and knoweth God. He that loveth not knoweth not God; for God is love. (1Jn 4:7-8 KJV)

This portion of scripture is one the most comprehensive summaries of Love. Love originates from God and nowhere else; He is the source of Love. He is our Father, we are born of Love, and His seed in us is Love. Anyone who says they know God is a loving person that is they know Love and practice it. Anyone who does not practice Love is not a child of God. We are known by Love.

Let's look at the word used as know in the Greek;

G1097

γινώσκω

ginōskō

ghin-oce'-ko

A prolonged form of a primary verb; to "know" (absolutely), in a great variety of applications and with many implications (as shown at left, with others not thus clearly expressed): - allow, be aware (of), feel, (have) known (-ledge), perceive, be resolved, can speak, be sure, understand.

Re; Strong's Dictionary

To know someone is to be aware, sure, understand and be conscious of someone's behavior and character. This is only possible by a deep relationship with that person or of course divine revelation by the Holy Ghost. The error is many people say they know someone based on their observations of their behavior not an intimate relationship with them. The same goes with people's knowledge of God it can be based on other people's experiences with God.

The message here is anyone who says they know God is saying they have an intimate relationship with Him. Anyone with an intimate relationship with God will be more like Him. So there is no need to investigate whether someone has a close relationship with the Lord. We just see your fruit, your character, how you deal with people and live your life. This will show if you are born of God and know Him.

Can two walk together, except they be agreed?
(Amo 3:3 KJV)

"Birds of a feather flock together". Is it possible for two people to spend a lot of time together except they have something in common? No it's impossible they cannot. Maybe for a short period people may have to deal with each other but eventually they will separate. That wonderful saying; "birds of a feather flock together". When you see a flock of birds they are all the same so it is with people. It also implies that anyone who says they are walking with God is in agreement with Him and will be like Him.

It is impossible to have a relationship with Jesus and not

be impacted by Love. The bible says God is Love. When we are born again we are children of Love. Jesus said the whole world will know we are His disciples by our Love for each other. Every Christian has the divine nature of Love in them. It is only corrupted by the thorns of the devil which enter through sin, bitterness and un-forgiveness. As long as we keep Jesus as Lord we are not just born of Love but obedient to Love. The fault comes when someone born of God is disobedient to God. This shows that although someone is born of Love they can be disobedient to Love.

That if you confess with your mouth, "Jesus is Lord," and believe in your heart that God raised him from the dead, you will be saved.
(Rom 10:9 NIV)

And why call ye me, Lord, Lord, and do not the things which I say?
(Luk 6:46 KJV).

Salvation comes by confessing Jesus as your Lord. From here we can say God's DNA is in your Spirit. However you must get to know God and follow His ways. In the same way a child has to get to know their parents and follow their rules to live under their roof. I'm sure you've seen an adopted child who has a similar character of their foster parents. Knowing and following your Father God is critical.

A prodigal child is at times disowned by their parents. Their rebellious life causes the parents to say even though you are from us you do not behave like us therefore we don't see you as a part of us. The Word of God reveals to us that it is not just saying Jesus is Lord that counts but keeping Him as your Lord.

Dear friends, let us love one another, for love comes from God. Everyone who loves has been born of God and knows God. (1Jn 4:7 NIV)

To be born of God and to know God is what matters. Your Love is the evidence that you know Him. Study anyone in the bible who knew God with intensity. We see the character of Love in them. For an example Moses and David were willing to take the punishment themselves and have the people spared.

As I've explained before Love is not just doing everything to make someone feel comfortable and happy. Love also has correction which someone void of wisdom will interpret as evil and hate. As you get to know who Love is you will perfect those traits in your character. There is a Spirit of excellence that is in every child of God that will be seen by Love. Just follow Jesus and His word step by step and you will be practicing Love.

Declaration

I declare that Jesus Christ is Lord of my life. I am born of God and know God. Every day I am getting to know God more and more. I am perfected by Love and this is seen by my Love in action in Jesus name. Amen

To be born of God and to know God is what matters. Your Love is the evidence that you know Him. Study anyone in the bible who knew God with intensity. We see the character of Love in them.

Constrained By Love – Day 11

For the love of Christ constraineth us; because we thus judge, that if one died for all, then were all dead: (2Co 5:14 KJV)

The wisdom of God is Him putting His Word within His children. The Love of God is in the hearts of His children. As a born again believer this Love constrains you. That means it holds you back and limits what you can do. Constraints for an example can be the constraints of a budget for a project. A project can be constrained by a budget. The expenditure has to stay within the budget limitations. In the same way the Love of God in us prevents us from stepping outside of the boundaries of God's Love.

Whatever we do, it is because Christ's love controls us. Since we believe that Christ died for everyone, we also believe that we have all died to the old life we used to live. (2Co 5:14 NLT)

We are held back and limited from doing certain things because of the Love of God in us as children of God. We are hedged in and bound by God's Love; it is like a fence or boundary that we cannot overstep. When dealing with those who have sinned for an example we deal with them in Love. Love corrects but seeks to restore and not destroy. The Love of God in our hearts prevents us from over stepping the boundaries of correction. When one steps outside of what they know is the limit they will be using the wrath of man.

Brethren, if a man be overtaken in a fault, ye which are spiritual, restore such an one in the spirit of meekness; considering thyself, lest thou also be tempted. (Gal 6:1 KJV)

For the wrath of man worketh not the righteousness of God. (Jas 1:20 KJV)

We see Jesus being angry at those who sold sacrifices in the Temple. The Gospels of Matthew, Mark and Luke record that Jesus drove out the moneychangers and those who sold sacrifices with their animals. These scriptures don't state that He beat up or whipped the people. Majority of Christians because of movies and wrong teachings believe that Jesus used His whip to thrash the people. I don't believe Jesus lashed the people with the whip. I believe He used it to drive the animals out. Maybe one or two dealers got caught in the cross fire but it isn't clearly stated in the scriptures.

And when he had made a scourge of small cords, he drove them all out of the temple, and the sheep, and the oxen; and poured out the changers' money, and overthrew the tables; And said unto them that sold doves, Take these things hence; make not my Father's house an house of merchandise. (Joh 2:15-16 KJV)

The point I'm making is that Jesus being the Love of God did not over step the limits to discipline. Some parents release all their anger and frustration on their children going beyond the limits of correction which is wrong. Even those who run prisons break the rules of discipline mistreating prisoners. Remember a prison is a correctional facility. Even the world knows discipline is about correction and restoration of offenders.

Furthermore we have had fathers of our flesh which corrected *us*, and we gave *them* reverence: shall we not much rather be in subjection unto the Father of spirits, and live? For they verily for a few days chastened *us* after their own pleasure; but he for *our* profit, that *we* might be partakers of his holiness. (Heb 12:9-10 KJV)

As Christians and Church leaders we must not break the limitations the Holy Spirit gives us when exercising judgment and correction. We must not be too lenient or too harsh. It must be controlled by the Love of Christ.

We are ruled by the love of Christ, now that we recognize that one man died for everyone, which means that they all share in his death. He died for all, so that those who live should no longer live for themselves, but only for him who died and was raised to life for their sake. (2Co 5:14-15 GNB)

The Love of Christ constrains us and brings us to the realization that we have to live our lives for Jesus. To live for Jesus is to live like Jesus.

This is my commandment, That ye love one another, as I have loved you. (Joh 15:12 KJV)

What a carnal Christian refers to as a conscience is the Love of God that put limits and boundaries in our hearts. This therefore also limits our speech and actions. It is not only a constraint when someone is at your mercy but also when showing grace towards others. The Love of Christ limits you and keeps you in this area where you feel moved to help people.

I have shewed you all things, how that so labouring ye ought to support the weak, and to remember the words of the Lord Jesus, how he said, It is more blessed to give than to receive.
(Act 20:35 KJV)

The Kingdom of God is where you live and the Love of God keeps you in this boundary. There is a way you live life. Even in your personal life you will know the limits. If you step further in a certain action you feel you are being pulled back. A step further you know is outside the boundary of Love and a step into sin. What causes this? It is the Love of God with His commands written on your heart by the Spirit of God.

This is why even a newly saved Christian has an in built understanding of what is right and wrong to a certain extent. Before someone is born again they are a sinner and don't see the sin in their life. The moment they are born again they have a "change of heart" and see the wrong in their life and are convicted to stop it. This is the Love of Christ constraining them.

God's Love keeps us from committing sin. I can liken it to rail road tracks and a train. The train is limited to where it can go by the railway line. If the train decides it wants to go somewhere outside of the railway tracks it will not make it. In the railways this is known as a derailment; when the train is off the railway line. Any Christian who obeys the railway line of Love remains on track. But a

Christian who decides to disobey the railway line on Love derails themselves from God's Will.

Some have refused to let their faith guide their conscience and their faith has been destroyed like a wrecked ship. (1Ti 1:19 GW)

Whatever is not of faith is sin and faith works by Love. If you see yourself going off track get back on track. God's guiding Love is there for your benefit.

Act

Submit to God and His Love. Resist the devil and disobedience to God.

We are hedged in and bound by God's Love; it is like a fence or boundary that we cannot overstep.

Faith Works By Love – Day 12

For in Jesus Christ neither circumcision availeth any thing, nor uncircumcision; but faith which worketh by love. (Gal 5:6 KJV)

The law is often seen by people as all those religious commands given by Moses. They fail to understand that the law is also put forth in different ways. For an example when a doctor or nutritionist tells you what to eat and what not to eat to be healthy. This is a law and is contrary to faith in Jesus Christ. It is based on fear; the fear that you will get a sickness if you don't eat accordingly. Likewise when someone is told unless you work you will not get money. In the world this can be seen as wisdom. It is earthly wisdom and does not apply to a child of God.

But if ye be led of the Spirit, ye are not under the law. (Gal 5:18 KJV)

Anything that brings fear is not of God. The opposite of Love is fear. The opposite of the law is grace. The opposite of faith in God is not just doubt but faith in someone or something else. You must either choose to trust God and His word or trust someone or something else. To trust someone or something else is doubt. The law tells you what you must do whereas grace enables you to do. Now then faith works by Love. That means trust in God works by God who is Love. Simply put the only way to trust in God is to be guided by the Holy Spirit.

For if you live according to the flesh you will die; but if by the Spirit you put to death the deeds of the body, you will live. For as many as are led by the Spirit of God, these are sons of God.
(Rom 8:13-14 NKJV)

The law which also includes mans carnal wisdom will tell you to do this and do that. Is it what God requires of you? No. God is saying what will benefit you is trust in Him which is driven by Love. As we have learnt earlier in this book all of the law is fulfilled in two commandments; Love God and Love your neighbour as yourself. Don't get caught up in the, is this thing law or faith question. Each person has a level of faith and should live by it. The examples I gave earlier concerning food and money can be different for someone whose faith is weak. Just know that faith can only be driven by Love. Whatever is not driven by Love is not of God.

But he who doubts is condemned if he eats, because he does not eat from faith; for whatever is not from faith is sin. (Rom 14:23 NKJV)

When we look through Hebrews chapter eleven which lists the heroes of faith; there is one thing common will all of them. They all trusted in the Lord with Love as the fuel to make them do what they did. These people all had reverence for the Lord. Likewise whatever you do in life as a child of God let it be fueled by Love.

Whoever says they are trusting in God is trusting in Love. This means your actions are Holy Ghost led. You cannot sin nor do evil to anyone when your faith is working by Love. Any faith (trust) that is driven by something other than Love is not faith in God and will result in the wrong fruit. All sin is trust in fear. A person lies because of fear of the truth exposing them. A person steals because of fear that they don't have what they want or need. A person can kill someone for fear of that person exposing them or killing them. All actions of sin are driven by fear. As children of God we are driven by Love and our trust in God who is Love.

For whatsoever *is* not of faith is sin.
(Rom 14:23b KJV)

Sin is the breaking of the law. Love is the fulfilling of the law. Anger is not of faith neither is it driven by Love. Bitterness and un-forgiveness is not trust in God driven by Love. These are examples of things driven by trust in the devil all about fear. A Christian who wants to be right will not be humble and forgive. It takes Love to suffer wrong and say ok let's just reconcile and let it go.

All strife is not a work of Love but fear which is faith in the devil. All wars started around the world are a result of fears driven by the devil. The fear of a people thinking they can never be free or possess their land or certain wealth has caused many wars.

As God's beloved child remain sensitive to the Spirit of God. Keep your heart soft and receptive to God's Love. As you do this you will fulfill what Jesus requires of you. There will be no strife or evil in your heart. There will be no room for the devil to work in you.

And they that are Christ's have crucified the flesh with the affections and lusts. If we live in the Spirit, let us also walk in the Spirit. Let us not be desirous of vain glory, provoking one another, envying one another. (Gal 5:24-26 KJV)

Declaration

I declare that I trust in the Lord Jesus and His Word. Everything I do in life is empowered by the Love of God. I submit to the Holy Spirit to lead my actions in Jesus name. Amen

For more on Faith read Forty Days On Faith by Jason Pullen

Now then faith works by Love. That means trust in God works by God who is Love.

All strife is not a work of Love but fear which is faith in the devil. All wars started around the world are a result of fears driven by the devil.

The Debt Of Love – Day 13

Owe no man any thing, but to love one another: for he that loveth another hath fulfilled the law.
(Rom 13:8 KJV)

The scripture above proves to us that Love is never ending; it is eternal. We are to owe no man anything but Love. At times this scripture has been wrongly taken to say one should never at all costs be in debt. I believe it is not directly saying one should never be in debt or that debt or borrowing is a sin. In the Old Testament a woman was told to borrow many vessels. At the same time the Prophet of God performed a miracle to retrieve an axe head that was borrowed. The emphasis of this verse is to always have a debt of Love.

Let love be your only debt! If you love others, you have done all that the Law demands.
(Rom 13:8 CEV)

When we have a debt of Love to everyone it means we always have to pay people with Love. Whenever someone is in debt they are constantly thinking of clearing the debt.

Please understand the context. The Lord is not saying never be in debt neither am I saying debt is good. The point we are driving through is that we must be conscious of owing everyone Love. It means when you think of your neighbour you think I owe them. When you think of your boss, pastor, relative and even your enemy, remember you owe them. Love is what you owe them.

Pay all your debts, except the debt of love for others. You can never finish paying that! If you love your neighbor, you will fulfill all the requirements of God's law. (Rom 13:8 NLT)

Can you imagine if everyone in the world walked around thinking like this? Everyone will be thinking and planning how to pay all they come in contact with Love. There is wisdom in the instructions from the Lord. There is a spiritual law of sowing and reaping. It implies that as you have it in your heart to pay Love to all, you will reap a harvest of Love. At the same don't make this a law that binds you in guilt if you don't show Love to everyone. The important thing is to have it in your heart that as a child of God you are in debt forever to all with Love.

And the most important piece of clothing you must wear is love. Love is what binds us all together in perfect harmony. (Col 3:14 NLT)

Love will never produce evil. Love always produces good fruit towards someone. It is not who you know that you should Love. It is also not only those who do good things to you that you should Love. The gospel tells us to Love all including our enemies.

"And if you lend to those from whom you hope to receive back, what credit is that to you? For even sinners lend to sinners to receive as much back. "But love your enemies, do good, and lend, hoping for nothing in return; and your reward will be great, and you will be sons of the Most High. For He is kind to the unthankful and evil. (Luk 6:34-35 NKJV)

In this bible verse Jesus spoke about lending and loving. If He instructed His disciples to lend it means Jesus approves of borrowing. Notice however Jesus said lend and don't do it expecting anything in return. He was saying borrow but don't do it expecting interest on your money or even your money back! Jesus was giving a revelation that we should Love and not do it expecting Love in return from that particular individual. God is the one who will pay back your acts of Love.

"But when you give a feast, invite the poor, the maimed, the lame, the blind. "And you will be blessed, because they cannot repay you; for you shall be repaid at the resurrection of the just." (Luk 14:13-14 NKJV)

Most people do favours and show Love to people who Love them or who they know can return the favour. In business they speak about your network of connections. Your network is your net-worth they say. There is little or no net-worth increase one will get from connecting with the poor, maimed, lame and blind. However you are connecting to the master King Jesus.

If you help the poor, you are lending to the LORD— and he will repay you! (Pro 19:17 NLT)

Confession

I acknowledge that I have a debt of Love to all. I confess that by the power of the Holy Ghost I will pay Love always in Jesus name. Amen

The important thing is to have it in your heart that as a child of God you are in debt forever to all with Love.

Love The Fruit – Day 14

But the fruit of the Spirit is love, joy, peace, longsuffering, gentleness, goodness, faith,
(Gal 5:22 KJV)

Fruit comes from plants. It is natural for trees to produce fruit according to the type of plant it is. The Spirit of God produces fruit as well. The fruits that the Holy Spirit produces are all stated below.

But the fruit of the Spirit is love, joy, peace, longsuffering, gentleness, goodness, faith, Meekness, temperance: against such there is no law.
(Gal 5:22-23 KJV)

There are nine fruits of the Spirit given. A child of God who yields to the Holy Spirit ought to produce these nine fruits. The first fruit of the Spirit is Love. All the other eight fruits are byproducts of Love. In my book New Believers' Foundation I brought this revelation. Love is the fruit of the Spirit, all the other fruits joy, peace, gentleness, goodness, faith, meekness and temperance are a form of Love in action. This is why there is no law against the fruit of the Spirit because there is no law against Love.

For this, Thou shalt not commit adultery, Thou shalt not kill, Thou shalt not steal, Thou shalt not bear false witness, Thou shalt not covet; and if *there be* any other commandment, it is briefly comprehended in this saying, namely, Thou shalt love thy neighbour as thyself. Love worketh no ill to his neighbour: therefore

love *is* the fulfilling of the law.
(Rom 13:9-10 KJV)

Jesus gave a teaching that people are like trees and can be known by their fruit. This He said is how you will know someone; by their fruit. Judas at one point appeared to be producing good fruit as he was part of the twelve who went out healing the sick and casting out devils. Saul at one point appeared to be bearing bad fruit as he went about arresting Christians and having them stoned. They both however "appeared to change" with Judas betraying Jesus and Saul serving Jesus with a name change to Paul. I say "appeared to change" because they actually did not change. One knew the Gospel and the other did not. We cannot judge someone until they've heard the Gospel and made their choice.

You can tell what they are by what they do. No one picks grapes or figs from thornbushes. A good tree produces good fruit, and a bad tree produces bad fruit. A good tree cannot produce bad fruit, and a bad tree cannot produce good fruit.
(Mat 7:16-18 CEV)

Love is fruit from a child of God. Judas was always a devil Jesus knew this but didn't reveal it. Jesus earlier on in His ministry only made it known that one of His disciples was a devil.

Jesus answered them, Have not I chosen you twelve, and one of you is a devil? (Joh 6:70 KJV)

Saul on the other hand ignorantly did evil. It was not who

he was he didn't know what he was doing. He had not yet heard the Gospel. We see this by what Jesus said about Saul even before Saul openly received the Gospel.

But the Lord said unto him, Go thy way: for he is a chosen vessel unto me, to bear my name before the Gentiles, and kings, and the children of Israel:
(Act 9:15 KJV)

When someone hears the Gospel, they encounter Jesus and have an opportunity to repent. Those who reject the Gospel reject Jesus and confirm the type of tree they are and want to be. A good tree repents when they hear the Gospel a bad tree doesn't change even when they hear the Gospel. Saul changed when he heard the Gospel.

And I thank Christ Jesus our Lord, who hath enabled me, for that he counted me faithful, putting me into the ministry; Who was before a blasphemer, and a persecutor, and injurious: but I obtained mercy, because I did *it* ignorantly in unbelief.
(1Ti 1:12-13 KJV)

Judas did not change even as a preacher and demonstrator of the Gospel with the twelve. Jesus knew he was a bad tree despite the healing he did, he ultimately betrayed the master.

Then he called his twelve disciples together, and gave them power and authority over all devils, and to cure diseases. And he sent them to preach the kingdom of God, and to heal the sick. (Luk 9:1-2 KJV)

And they departed, and went through the towns, preaching the gospel, and healing every where. (Luk 9:6 KJV)

The fruit of Love is seen in what we produce. You do not need to try and produce this fruit. It is a reflection of who you are. A born again child of God must remain in submission to Jesus. This is what ensures you remain a good tree bearing good fruit.

And why call ye me, Lord, Lord, and do not the things which I say? (Luk 6:46 KJV)

The examples given above were to show you that it is not just working of miracles or preaching the Gospel that determines the fruit one is producing. King Jesus knows who is following Him and therefore bearing the fruit of Love. We are trees planted by God it is our nature to produce kindness and affection.

To appoint unto them that mourn in Zion, to give unto them beauty for ashes, the oil of joy for mourning, the garment of praise for the spirit of heaviness; that they might be called trees of righteousness, the planting of the LORD, that he might be glorified. (Isa 61:3 KJV)

God is glorified when we bear good fruit. Someone may still be wondering about how Judas could bear bad fruit while being so close to Jesus. Remember we must remain obedient to Jesus. When we do this we stay connected to God. If someone is disobedient to God it means they are obedient to the devil. The doing of the good things of

God is directly connected to God. As Jesus said He is the vine and we are the branches.

"I am the vine, you are the branches. He who abides in Me, and I in him, bears much fruit; for without Me you can do nothing. "If anyone does not abide in Me, he is cast out as a branch and is withered; and they gather them and throw them into the fire, and they are burned. (Joh 15:5-6 NKJV)

Keep yourself submissive to the Spirit of God. By doing this, you remain connected to your Father, your source and are connected to the vine. God has chosen you to hold the fruit. This is what a branch does. But never forget that the source of the fruit is the vine. This will keep you humble as you do miraculous things for God.

Declaration

I declare that I am a tree of righteousness planted by the Lord. I am a branch of Jesus. I remain obedient to my source. I am connected to the vine and produce the fruit of Love naturally in Jesus name. Amen

The first fruit of the Spirit is Love. All the other eight fruits are byproducts of Love.

Labour Of Love – Day 15

Remembering without ceasing your work of faith, and labour of love, and patience of hope in our Lord Jesus Christ, in the sight of God and our Father; Knowing, brethren beloved, your election of God.
(1Th 1:3-4 KJV)

Many people all over the world get up every day and go to work. I recall one time in Asia speaking with a friend of mines employee, his English was not that good but better than the rest. In fact I often used him to communicate with my friend. He asked me a question about how much a "labourer" earns in my home country. I knew he meant general work or manual work. I laughed alone later at his expression "labourer". Soon after that however the Holy Ghost brought the revelation to me in a different way of being His labourer!

We give thanks to God always for you all, making mention of you in our prayers; Remembering without ceasing your work of faith, and labour of love, and patience of hope in our Lord Jesus Christ, in the sight of God and our Father; (1Th 1:2-3 KJV)

In most nations a labourer is one who does the hard work, manual labour. These jobs are often given to prisoners or offenders as community service. To work the fields in the heat and other such jobs.

Doing the "dirty work" in developing nations doesn't pay well. In certain developed nations with much better economies however manual labour pays well. Why you might wonder? This is because the majority of people if given a choice don't want to do the dirty work. Hard labour is seen as a lowly job. Slaves not masters used to do such jobs.

Our above portion of scripture was making reference to all those in Thessalonica that were believers. Meaning all of them worked in faith, laboured in Love and were patient in hope.

As a child of God you know that you have a debt of Love to pay. At the same time there is the labour of Love. This is a job given to every Christian it can be like working a field on a hot day or taking out the rubbish. It's the dirty work that no one likes to do but it has to be done; to show Love to all. This is not easy. It takes some effort to Love people. The preaching of the Gospel is not just the duty of Apostles, Prophets, Pastors, Evangelists, Bishops, Deacons and Church leaders. It is the duty of all born again Christians.

And this commandment we have from Him: that he who loves God must love his brother also. (1Jn 4:21 NKJV)

The bible shows us that as lovers of God we also must be lovers of our brothers. A brother is someone close, a relative. I can say your family. As it is often said you cannot choose your family. There is a bond with family that cannot be easily broken. We are expected to show Love to those closest to us first before loving the general public. Brotherly kindness comes before charity.

To godliness brotherly kindness, and to brotherly kindness love. (2Pe 1:7 NKJV)

It is foolish and against God's order to feed a community when you haven't fed your immediate family first! It can be hard work to Love family. You may not agree on issues, faith and so on. We still have to Love our family members. This is a labour of Love. At times family members try their best to avoid each other and only meet at major family events. Avoidance like this is so that one doesn't have to tolerate or make an effort to Love certain relatives they don't get on with. Tolerating also isn't Love.

When you are in constant contact with someone you know them for longer, this is when Love is put to the test. A married couple for an example knows the good, bad and ugly about each other. There must be the labour of Love to keep a successful marriage. Both parties have to learn to forgive and work Love to each other.

Then we are also told to Love our neighbours and enemies!

Ye have heard that it hath been said, Thou shalt love thy neighbour, and hate thine enemy. But I say unto you, Love your enemies, bless them that curse you, do good to them that hate you, and pray for them which despitefully use you, and persecute you;
(Mat 5:43-44 KJV)

With family there is little choice in having them in your life. With neighbours, the general public and enemies we have a choice. We can choose to avoid, block and stay away at all costs. By distancing from someone you cannot Love them. Please understand this doesn't mean you have to have everyone in your life. The word of God tells us to have no relations at all with certain people. God can also tell you to cast someone out of your life. We have no fellowship with devils or evil.

As a Christian, remember you have some work to do in loving people. Winning a soul can be very easy or it can be hard labour. At times we've gone to preach in rural areas costing time, resources, damage to cars, equipment and more. Then we arrive at a place and face a hostile crowd. After much effort we see salvations at the end. One could have very easily said Jesus said shake off the dust and move on. But Love causes you to endure and show mercy so that grace can work. Love is a choice.

The Lord revealed to me a way of seeing the power of Love in a person is how long they have kept relationships. The longer a relationship the more tests it goes through. A faithful person shows Love. This is why modern Christianity has people who can easily be a part of five different churches in four years. When they find a rift somewhere they simply jump ship. Or the other option is to be involved but not too involved, avoiding getting too close. That is not Love.

For God *is* not unrighteous to forget your work and labour of love, which ye have shewed toward his name, in that ye have ministered to the saints, and do minister. (Heb 6:10 KJV)

It must be known the type of laboring we are speaking of here. The labour of Love in the Gospel! It pays to serve God! When you stretch yourself and exercise Love for His sake you are serving God. Know that He is a rewarder of His servants. He is not unrighteous to forget your overtime! He remembers and rewards. Rightfully be expectant to receive from King Jesus as you actively Love people with the Gospel.

So Jesus answered and said, "Assuredly, I say to you, there is no one who has left house or brothers or sisters or father or mother or wife or children or lands, for My sake and the gospel's, "who shall not receive a hundredfold now in this time; houses and brothers and sisters and mothers and children and lands, with persecutions; and in the age to come, eternal life. (Mar 10:29-30 NKJV)

All your effort to demonstrate the Love of the Gospel to people will be rewarded here on earth and in the time to come. The labour of Love is necessary for the Salvation of souls. The Apostle Paul whose works are still blessing many today had to endure. A woman when giving birth is termed to be "in labour". The labour of Love of the Gospel can be painful but it certainly births eternal beauty. Paul listed some of his labour of Love.

Are they ministers of Christ?; I speak as a fool; I am more: in labors more abundant, in stripes above measure, in prisons more frequently, in deaths often. (2Co 11:23 NKJV)

Jesus Christ's labour of Love was death by carrying our sins.

Looking unto Jesus, the author and finisher of our faith, who for the joy that was set before Him endured the cross, despising the shame, and has sat down at the right hand of the throne of God. (Heb 12:2 NKJV)

We reap what we sow as you labour in Love you will harvest the fruit of Love. Abel's works of Love still spoke when he was dead.

By faith Abel offered to God a more excellent sacrifice than Cain, through which he obtained witness that he was righteous, God testifying of his gifts; and through it he being dead still speaks. (Heb 11:4 NKJV)

Your works of Love will always remain. Even if people try and forget you, God will cause your name to be remembered. Many people who have made great sacrifices motivated by Love are remembered around the world and in history.

And I heard a voice from heaven saying unto me, Write, Blessed *are* the dead which die in the Lord from henceforth: Yea, saith the Spirit, that they may rest from their labours; and their works do follow them. (Rev 14:13 KJV)

Act

Labour in Love for Jesus and the Gospel's sake.

A woman when giving birth is termed to be "in labour". The labour of Love of the Gospel can be painful but it certainly births eternal beauty.

Prove Your Love – Day 16

This is a way to prove how true your love is.
(2Co 8:8b NLV)

In the natural world scientists have come up with various ways of testing for the presence of certain items. Whether it's to test what nutrients are contained in food or minerals in a rock; there are proven ways to test for these things. The word of God is the wisdom of God and also gives us truth on how to test qualities. Our opening verse shows how to test if Love is genuine or not. Let's see what exactly the Apostle Paul by divine revelation gave to the people of Corinth as a test of genuine Love.

Since you excel in so many ways—you have so much faith, such gifted speakers, such knowledge, such enthusiasm, and such love for us—now I want you to excel also in this gracious ministry of giving. I am not saying you must do it, even though the other churches are eager to do it. This is one way to prove your love is real. (2Co 8:7-8 NLT)

The church in Corinth had shown some good traits acknowledged by Paul and Titus who was sent to them. However Paul said in as much as that is good, their Love needed to be proven to be real. A way of proving Love is by the ministry of giving! This is the wisdom of God, a test for Love. When someone says they Love as we have defined Love, they will give. A person who is obedient in all other things but cannot give does not Love.

This is the "litmus test" for Love, your giving. Do you Love God? We don't need to be told that, the proof will be in your giving to God. How do you give to God? By paying your tithes to your church and giving offerings. Offerings include giving to ministers of the Gospel and the poor. This is where Love is seen. Paul said to the people you have shown willingness and a good attitude but now prove you are genuine.

Now therefore perform the doing *of it;* that as *there was* a readiness to will, so *there may be* a performance also out of that which ye have. For if there be first a willing mind, *it is* accepted according to that a man hath, *and* not according to that he hath not. (2Co 8:11-12 KJV)

It is good to speak well about your Love for Jesus, His Kingdom and so on. From the heart we speak but after that there must be action. The Lord wants Love to be shown by action and the action is giving money and material things. That which costs you something! We see the proof of Jesus' Love by leaving behind all His Glory, coming to earth, becoming poor on the cross by dying for us.

I do not speak according to command, but through the eagerness of others, and testing the trueness of your love. For you know the grace of our Lord Jesus Christ, that, though He was rich, for your sakes He became poor, in order that you might be made rich through His poverty. (2Co 8:8-9 MKJV)

The sacrificial Love of God is eternal. The scars of His Love are a sign of His compassion. The nail scars of Jesus did not disappear when He rose again. The holes in His hands are a mark of His Love for us. In this day and age some people tattoo the name of the one they Love on their body. The Lord has engraved our names in His hands!

See, I have engraved you on the palms of my hands; your walls are ever before me.
(Isa 49:16 NIV)

The message of Christianity is a revelation of Love through God's act of giving. Think on that for a moment. The message of Christianity is a revelation of Love through God's act of giving. The most translated and quoted bible verse that delivers the Gospel is about the proof of God's Love demonstrated by sacrificial giving.

For God so loved the world that He gave His only-begotten Son, that whoever believes in Him should not perish but have everlasting life.
(Joh 3:16 MKJV)

God loved the world and proved His Love by giving. It was not just small giving but the greatest sacrifice in giving. His one and only son, He did it to reap a harvest of sons. Whoever accepts His Love becomes His son. This is bringing another revelation; that Love brings multiplication.

But as many as received him, to them gave he power to become the sons of God, *even* **to them that believe on his name:** (Joh 1:12 KJV)

When we say we Love someone the truth of our Love is seen in our giving towards that person. The evidence of your genuine backing is in your support for the one you Love. Please understand I am not saying you should be taken advantage of and have others depend on you for everything while they remain idle. No!

The message is to prove that you Love someone or something there must be genuine giving towards that person or thing. When you see someone saying they Love you but never give a cent towards you, just know that is not Love. At the same time being given many things alone is not Love. Go back to day one of this book to get full understanding on this. The Spirit of God reveals that one's Love is seen in their giving. This is concerning money and material wealth. These give the measure of one's effort or work in the natural. Love is not just justified in prayer, fasting and other things which are good but there is a measure. The measure is that which costs you something.

Then the king said to Araunah, "No, but I will surely buy it from you for a price; nor will I offer burnt offerings to the LORD my God with that which costs me nothing." So David bought the threshing floor and the oxen for fifty shekels of silver.
(2Sa 24:24 NKJV)

And He looked up and saw the rich putting their gifts into the treasury, and He saw also a certain poor widow putting in two mites. So He said, "Truly I say to you that this poor widow has put in more than all;
(Luk 21:1-3 NKJV)

Jesus knows what costs you. This is why a tithe is a tenth of your increase. It's a test that you serve God. Jesus only compared himself with money. Judas the master of deceit who everyone thought was serving Jesus was actually serving money. Eventually Judas proved his Love for money by betraying Jesus for thirty pieces of silver. Judas only agreed to betray Jesus soon after an act of Love by the woman with the Alabaster Jar. The woman proved her Love for Jesus by giving what cost her. At the same time Judas proved himself by his response.

Verily I say unto you, Wheresoever this gospel shall be preached in the whole world, *there* shall also this, that this woman hath done, be told for a memorial of her. Then one of the twelve, called Judas Iscariot, went unto the chief priests, And said *unto them,* What will ye give me, and I will deliver him unto you? And they covenanted with him for thirty pieces of silver.
(Mat 26:13-15 KJV)

There are many sayings in the world which have been derived from biblical truth.
"Talk is cheap"
"Put your money where your mouth is"

The above two sayings mean it costs nothing to say something but talk must be backed by actions. At the same time if you say something back it up and do it. Faith without works is dead. If we say we Love God and people we must prove it. This was the message to the church in Corinth. They heard many good things about them but they had not given towards the work of God as they ought to. This is why Paul said prove your Love by backing the work of the Gospel.

If any questions are raised, remember that Titus is my partner and coworker to help you. The other men are representatives of the churches and bring glory to Christ. So give these men a demonstration of your love. Show their congregations that we were right to be proud of you. (2Co 8:23-24 GW)

Act
Prove your Love.

This is the "litmus test" for Love, your giving. Do you Love God? We don't need to be told that, the proof will be in your giving to God.

The message of Christianity is a revelation of Love through God's act of giving.

Love Rebukes & Corrects – Day 17

Better is open rebuke Than love that is concealed. Faithful are the wounds of a friend, But deceitful are the kisses of an enemy.
(Pro 27:5-6 NASB)

Open rebuke is better than secret Love. We are bringing the truth of Love in this book. That is true Love, the Love of God. One of the things which Love does is to rebuke and correct. Wherever there is Love there is an open rebuke for wrong doing and correction.

Against an elder receive not an accusation, but before two or three witnesses. Them that sin rebuke before all, that others also may fear. I charge *thee* before God, and the Lord Jesus Christ, and the elect angels, that thou observe these things without preferring one before another, doing nothing by partiality.
(1Ti 5:19-21 KJV)

The instruction of the Lord on correction is clear. It is for everyone in the body of Christ no one is outside of correction and rebuke. This does not mean a harsh disgrace of someone but highlighting the error of the person of high or low authority and restoring them.

Brethren, if a man be overtaken in a fault, ye which are spiritual, restore such an one in the spirit of meekness; considering thyself, lest thou also be tempted. (Gal 6:1 KJV)

Love does not destroy but creates. Thus when there is correction it is for salvation and restoration. When the Holy Ghost shows you an error of a beloved there is a way to bring rebuke or correction. When you are in a position to bring rebuke (when someone is under your authority) do so. If it is an elder who has done wrong (or someone not under your authority) correct them.

Rebuke not an elder, but intreat *him* **as a father;** *and* **the younger men as brethren; The elder women as mothers; the younger as sisters, with all purity.**
(1Ti 5:1-2 KJV)

The aim of Love is not to embarrass or prove a point but to keep the truth of God. If your leader sins or makes a mistake we are told to entreat them as a father. This means the way you speak to them matters. In an attitude of Love and respect you tell them privately first their mistake. If they hear you good, if not you are to bring one or two mature Christians and tell your leader their error. If they listen it's good if not you can then tell the church. If they don't hear the church then you are free of them.

The above can also apply if you are in a position of authority over someone. Correct in meekness.

"Moreover if your brother sins against you, go and tell him his fault between you and him alone. If he hears you, you have gained your brother. "But if he will not hear, take with you one or two more, that 'by the mouth of two or three witnesses every word may be established.' "And if he refuses to hear them, tell it to the church. But if he refuses even to hear the church, let him be to you like a heathen and a tax collector.

"Assuredly, I say to you, whatever you bind on earth will be bound in heaven, and whatever you loose on earth will be loosed in heaven. "Again I say to you that if two of you agree on earth concerning anything that they ask, it will be done for them by My Father in heaven. (Mat 18:15-19 NKJV)

The main reason people refuse to highlight someone's error or sin is fear. The bible never said just pray for your leader if they are wrong. No we are told to entreat our leaders when they are wrong. It can be like "the elephant in the room". The whole church knows their Pastor has a problem but no one would dare speak to him about it because they fear him. Or on the other hand a Pastor wouldn't dare correct his congregants for a mediocre attitude for fear they may leave the church.

As you can see in both cases fear is preventing Love from bringing correction. When there is Love there is correction openly. This is what Paul did to Peter when Peter did not walk in the truth of the Gospel.

But when Peter came to Antioch, I opposed him in public, because he was clearly wrong. Before some men who had been sent by James arrived there, Peter had been eating with the Gentile believers. But after these men arrived, he drew back and would not eat with the Gentiles, because he was afraid of those who were in favor of circumcising them. The other Jewish believers also started acting like cowards along with Peter; and even Barnabas was swept along by their cowardly action. When I saw that they were not walking a straight path in line with the truth of the gospel, I said to Peter in front of them all, "You are a Jew, yet you have been living like a Gentile, not like a

Jew. How, then, can you try to force Gentiles to live like Jews?" (Gal 2:11-14 GNB)

Apostle Paul at this point in time had a lower reputation in the church in authority as compared to Peter, yet Apostle Paul boldly rebuked Apostle Peter in public. This must be why King Jesus entrusted Paul with such great revelation. Paul was about Love in truth. I'm sure others would have said; Paul we can discuss this later, be peaceful, let it be. That would've been secret love.

Open rebuke *is* better than secret love. Faithful *are* the wounds of a friend; but the kisses of an enemy *are* deceitful. (Pro 27:5-6 KJV)

Secret Love is when someone see's the fault of someone but refuses to speak to the person about it. Majority of the time it is the Holy Ghost who will highlight someone's error to a person and say talk to them about it, rebuke them or correct them. When someone chooses to remain silent that is "secret Love". You have a labour of Love the Lord has given to you but you refuse to do it. This is where the misunderstanding of forgiveness, mercy, reconciliation and peace comes in. Let me explain.

Rebuke and correction is necessary even when there is forgiveness. You can forgive someone for their wrong doing but you do not neglect to tell them their wrong. Mercy must be allowed to function but it does not mean rebuke and correction is absent. There cannot be reconciliation until the judgment of the Spirit of God has been given. There cannot be peace until the truth as given by the Lord has been accepted. There is rebuke and correction in restoration, forgiveness, mercy and peace. You cannot turn a blind eye on errors. You cannot be the blind led by the blind!

Fake "love" is to hold back when the Holy Spirit prompts you to bring correction to someone. When it comes to elders in the Spirit (not age) you are not to rebuke but entreat. This is because we expect leaders to more often than not be in right standing. This is why I am putting emphasis on the prompting of the Holy Ghost. He will prompt you mostly to correct those He has given you authority over or those leaders who will listen to you. God is not the author of confusion. Please do not take this as license to go around bringing rebuke, be led by the Spirit. At the same time be ready to receive correction and rebuke when you have missed it. It is not hate but true Love.

And ye have forgotten the exhortation which speaketh unto you as unto children, My son, despise not thou the chastening of the Lord, nor faint when thou art rebuked of him: For whom the Lord loveth he chasteneth, and scourgeth every son whom he receiveth. (Heb 12:5-6 KJV)

Over the years some people have distanced from me because they did not like what I said to them as a check of correction. Some of these people have returned later and said thank you for that time you corrected me and they are still running. When they return at times I would've forgotten and they have to remind me what I said. This is because it was the Lord motivating me not my flesh or personal opinion. Others view the correction I gave as hate or "judgment".
(There is a difference between righteous judgment and

condemnation)

A loving friend, parent, pastor or leader corrects to prevent the downfall of someone. Even if the person may react or feel the correction is painful. Oh yes Love can bring pain. It is not an evil pain or physical pain but a righteous pain of rebuke and correction. Let this be clear God does not correct with evil, harm or sickness but with His Word.

Open rebuke *is* better than secret love. Faithful *are* the wounds of a friend; but the kisses of an enemy *are* deceitful. (Pro 27:5-6 KJV)

Correction can feel like a wound but it is for edification not destruction. The kisses of an enemy; is that person who wants to see forgiveness, reconciliation and peace without dealing with the matter, without acknowledging the wrong doer and correcting them. Jesus showed mercy but with truth and correction. We must do likewise.

A deceiver (the devil) comes with a kiss and says oh just let it go. They are living wrong but there is grace and mercy let them be at peace. No loving parent wants their child to escape their correction and land up in a government correctional facility; a prison!

If ye endure chastening, God dealeth with you as with sons; for what son is he whom the father chasteneth not? But if ye be without chastisement, whereof all are partakers, then are ye bastards, and not sons.
(Heb 12:7-8 KJV)

To remain as a legitimate child of God, receive His

correction. Likewise when you are led by the Holy Ghost to chastise whoever it might be do so in meekness. Whoever rejects God's correction cannot remain His child. Whoever refuses to repent believes they are right and are in danger of having their name blotted out of the Lambs book of life.

He that overcometh, the same shall be clothed in white raiment; and I will not blot out his name out of the book of life, but I will confess his name before my Father, and before his angels. (Rev 3:5 KJV)

As many as I love, I rebuke and chasten: be zealous therefore, and repent. (Rev 3:19 KJV)

Confession

I confess that I am subject to correction by my Heavenly Father as His child. I embrace His chastisement when He gives it for my perfection. I will not faint when the Lord rebukes and corrects me. I will be strengthened by His Love. I confess that I will give correction and rebuke without fear, compromise or partiality as led by the Holy Spirit in Jesus name. Amen

---

There is rebuke and correction in restoration, forgiveness, mercy and peace. You cannot turn a blind eye on errors. You cannot be the blind led by the blind!

The Jealousy Of Love – Day 18

So the angel that communed with me said unto me, Cry thou, saying, Thus saith the LORD of hosts; I am jealous for Jerusalem and for Zion with a great jealousy. (Zec 1:14 KJV)

It may come as a surprise to some who have read through the attributes of Love which states Love is not jealous or envious, to see the headline of today, the jealousy of Love.

Love is patient and kind. Love is not jealous or boastful or proud. (1Co 13:4 NLT)

It is always important to rightly divide the word of God that is to understand everything Gods word says in its proper context and meaning. Love itself does not show envy or jealousy to the one or thing it loves. However there is jealously because of Love. I will explain this.

First of all understand jealousy is similar to envy and intolerance. When we bring jealousy into the context of Love, we understand its place. It is not at all wrong. As in a Love relationship between a husband and wife, there is jealousy for anyone who tries to take their place in that relationship. This is different to someone who is jealous and envious for something that is not theirs, such as someone's material things, child or spouse. In that context jealousy is sinful. This is the tenth commandment given by Moses; do not desire that which is not yours.

" Do not have a desire for your neighbor's house. Do not have a desire for his wife or his male servant, his female servant, or his bull or his donkey or anything that belongs to your neighbor." (Exo 20:17 NLV)

The second commandment God gave Moses to the children of Israel came with a revelation attached to it. The first of the Ten Commandments is, have no other gods but God. The second is do not create any idol or god and worship it. This one came with a revelation let's read it below.

Thou shalt not make unto thee any graven image, or any likeness *of any thing* **that** *is* **in heaven above, or that** *is* **in the earth beneath, or that** *is* **in the water under the earth: Thou shalt not bow down thyself to them, nor serve them: for I the LORD thy God** *am* **a jealous God, visiting the iniquity of the fathers upon the children unto the third and fourth** *generation* **of them that hate me; And shewing mercy unto thousands of them that love me, and keep my commandments.** (Exo 20:4-6 KJV)

The Lord explained why the Israelites shouldn't have worshipped idols or other gods because He is a jealous God. This is where we get one of the names of God as Jehovah Qanna or El Qanna which means God is jealous.
This is the Hebrew word for jealous. (Qanna)

H7067

קַנָּא

qannâ'

kan-naw'

From H7065; *jealous*. - jealous. Compare H7072.

Re; Strongs dictionary

The Lord was making it known that He is jealous over anyone or anything that takes His place as God over His people Israel. This is why throughout the Old Testament we see the utter annihilation of Israel's enemies with Egypt who enslaved them as a prime example. When you look deeper into the plagues that came at the hand of Moses every one of them was against an Egyptian god.

As a child of God you are part of the church of Jesus Christ that is His wife. There is not only jealousy in a marriage relationship but even in children including children of the faith. We see the Apostle Paul telling the Saints he taught how jealous he was over them with godly jealousy. He did not want to see those he raised in the truth become corrupted by any wrong teaching.

For I am jealous over you with godly jealousy: for I have espoused you to one husband, that I may present *you as* **a chaste virgin to Christ. But I fear, lest by any means, as the serpent beguiled Eve through his subtilty, so your minds should be corrupted from the simplicity that is in Christ. For if he that cometh preacheth**

another Jesus, whom we have not preached, or *if* ye receive another spirit, which ye have not received, or another gospel, which ye have not accepted, ye might well bear with *him.* (2Co 11:2-4 KJV)

There is a right place for jealousy. The Apostle made it clear that he did not own anyone but he made those he taught understand the kind of love he had for them. He was not just going to allow a deceiver to come in and take the flock of God he had kept. As a Pastor or church leader never just let anyone corrupt those God has given you to watch over. They have a choice but you have a duty to watch over them jealously.

Be thou diligent to know the state of thy flocks, *and* look well to thy herds. (Pro 27:23 KJV)

Be shepherds of God's flock that is under your care, serving as overseers--not because you must, but because you are willing, as God wants you to be; not greedy for money, but eager to serve; not lording it over those entrusted to you, but being examples to the flock. (1Pe 5:2-3 NIV)

Jealousy can bring out the fight in a person. I've witnessed boyfriends go after any guy they suspect of being after their woman and vice versa. I've seen mothers threaten men or institutions way more powerful than them standing in jealous Love for their child.
I once had a lesson from the Lord when I was puzzled by the behavior of my one dog. He would charge aggressively at the other dogs and I didn't know why. As I tried to see the pattern, I noticed he did it every time I carried or patted another dog. Even the dog way bigger

than him, he would attack. There and then the Lord spoke to me and said he is jealous for you. I was stunned. Then I remembered how much closer and more obedient he always was to me. This brought me to the remembrance of the Lord's jealousy over us as His children. He doesn't want anyone or anything coming in between our relationship with Him. Whether it's your Love for your pets, career, business, children, calling, church or even your spouse! Nothing must take the place of Jesus in your life.

Set me as a seal upon thine heart, as a seal upon thine arm: for love *is* strong as death; jealousy *is* cruel as the grave: the coals thereof *are* coals of fire, *which hath a* most vehement flame. (Son 8:6 KJV)

The Love God has for you as an individual is fierce and as strong as death. This is why He says don't revenge for yourself but let me deal with your enemies. It is a fearful thing to fall into the hands of the living God. He is amazingly merciful but let no one touch His beloved bride that would be it for them.

Dearly beloved, avenge not yourselves, but *rather* give place unto wrath: for it is written, Vengeance *is* mine; I will repay, saith the Lord. (Rom 12:19 KJV)

Declaration

I declare that I am dearly beloved by Jesus Christ. The Lord my maker is jealous for me. I am the apple of His eye. Whatever or whoever tries to come against me or between my relationship with Jesus is in danger of the wrath of almighty God.

He doesn't want anyone or anything coming in between our relationship with Him. Whether it's your Love for your pets, career, business, children, calling, church or even your spouse! Nothing must take the place of Jesus in your life.

Love Gives Meaning - Day 19

But eagerly desire the greater gifts. And now I will show you the most excellent way.
(1Co 12:31 NIV)

For something to have value it must have purpose and meaning or else it is a waste. There must be a reason behind all things. Why do people do what they do? What is the motivation behind them? Whenever someone is passionate about something they do it with excellence, diligence and to the best of their ability. We can say they Love what they do! If there is no Love there is no meaning.

Are all apostles? Are all prophets? Are all teachers? Do all work miracles? Do all have gifts of healing? Do all speak in tongues? Do all interpret? But eagerly desire the greater gifts. And now I will show you the most excellent way. (1Co 12:29-31 NIV)

The Apostle Paul broke down various gifts and callings of the Lord. Then he said there is a more excellent way. What is that way, the very next verse explains it.

If I speak in the tongues of men and of angels, but have not love, I am only a resounding gong or a clanging cymbal. (1Co 13:1 NIV)

Without Love we are nothing. Love is the more excellent way that gives you meaning and a purpose. When something is done backed by Love there is value and purpose especially on the person doing whatever it is they may be doing. There is a reward for the doer. If great and mighty things are done without Love they are still powerful but whoever did it has no meaning or value.

If I have the gift of prophecy and can fathom all mysteries and all knowledge, and if I have a faith that can move mountains, but have not love, I am nothing. (1Co 13:2 NIV)

Note Apostle Paul said if he moves mountains without Love he is nothing. The act of moving the mountain remains great but done without Love he has no meaning and value. God is Love therefore when you do something with Love you are testifying that you are doing it inspired by God. Anything done without God truly has no life because life is from God. When there is Love there is life.

And whatsoever ye do, do *it* heartily, as to the Lord, and not unto men; Knowing that of the Lord ye shall receive the reward of the inheritance: for ye serve the Lord Christ. (Col 3:23-24 KJV)

When you do all things as if you are doing them for the Lord I believe you will be doing your best. Doing things with a good attitude and concern shows Love. When the Lord created the heavens and the earth He was pleased and saw that it was good. You can see Love at work in creation. This is why some people even begin to worship creatures or nature. They are blind to the creator but go on worshipping what He made.

The details and excellence in creation, science, biology, astronomy and all other fields reveal the excellence of the

Lord. His excellence is simply Love. There is a meaning behind every star, planet, animal and so on. They all tell a story about the Love of God. All of creation has purpose, value and meaning because of God who is Love.

How clearly the sky reveals God's glory! How plainly it shows what he has done! Each day announces it to the following day; each night repeats it to the next.
(Psa 19:1-2 GNB)

The sun has meaning because of Love not because it is the sun. Life is dependent upon the sun. An ant has meaning not because it is an ant but because of Love. It is Love that gives all things meaning. If Love is removed there is no life and there is no meaning. This is why it is essential to live for God. When you do this you will continue living. People lose hope when they lose a purpose for living. It is not the sickness, disease, age or the devil that ends someone's life it is a person's loss of the desire to live. Maintain a desire to live for God and you will keep on living.

Faith without works is dead. It is important to understand that it is faith in God. Trust in God. Trust in Love. This is why the bible tells us that even a sacrificial act without Love does not benefit the person. If Jesus did not Love people and just went to the cross because the Father told Him to, Jesus would not have received the reward of a name above all names.

If I gave everything I have to the poor and even sacrificed my body, I could boast about it; but if I didn't love others, I would be of no value whatsoever.
(1Co 13:3 NLT)

The key to adding value, purpose and meaning to your life is Love! Do all things with Love for God and you will enjoy life and understand its meaning.

But if I do it gladly, I have a reward; and if not, I am under orders to do it. (1Co 9:17 BBE)

Our Heavenly Father wants us to do what we do with Love as the driving force. Faith works by Love. With Love as our fuel we will be rewarded for our actions. God desires to reward you. The greatest act of Love is to die for someone. Jesus did this and received a name above every other name.

Let this mind be in you which was also in Christ Jesus, (Php 2:5 NKJV)

And being found in appearance as a man, He humbled Himself and became obedient to the point of death, even the death of the cross. Therefore God also has highly exalted Him and given Him the name which is above every name, (Php 2:8-9 NKJV)

Confession

I confess that I will not just do things for the sake of doing them. I understand that Love gives everything meaning. Therefore I will do all things by Love with the help of the Holy Spirit in Jesus name. Amen

Anything done without God truly has no life because life is from God. When there is Love there is life.

It is Love that gives all things meaning. If Love is removed there is no life and there is no meaning. This is why it is essential to live for God.

Love Is A Fire – Day 20

Place me like a seal over your heart, like a seal on your arm; for love is as strong as death, its jealousy unyielding as the grave. It burns like blazing fire, like a mighty flame. Many waters cannot quench love; rivers cannot wash it away. If one were to give all the wealth of his house for love, it would be utterly scorned. (Son 8:6-7 NIV)

Fire has amazing attributes. It brings heat, light, warmth, purification and more. Christians at times only see fire as wrath and judgment. The Love of God is also seen as fire. It is a good fire. God and His word cannot be separated. His word is also seen as a fire. God's Love is a fire that cannot be quenched.

Is not my word like as a fire? saith the LORD; and like a hammer *that* breaketh the rock in pieces? Therefore, behold, I *am* against the prophets, saith the LORD, that steal my words every one from his neighbour. (Jer 23:29-30 KJV)

God's word is His Love. It is a fire. This why Jesus said He came to set fire on earth but the fire was already kindled. What did He mean? He meant He was increasing the zeal and Love for God which was already there. Some ministers of God shout fire when ministering not knowing why. They just do it, perhaps they were prompted but others just copied someone else. Our verse above tells us God's word is a fire and that He is against prophets who steal words from another and say "God said". This is dangerous but common and popular in the information age. A minister just searches on the internet what a well known prophet has said and begins to parrot it. Others search for sermons and preach them or copy another revelation and put it in a book. That is not right. I believe ministers can learn and hear from other ministers but not to purport as thou it was their revelation. God doesn't like hypocrisy. If you heard it or learnt it somewhere just give credit there. As a minister, be led by Jesus never say the Lord said to you such and such if He didn't. So why do ministers shout fire?

This first came to my attention when I was a young Christian and a Prophet of God (Prophet Collin) asked me a question. His words would always carry weight. At one time he said to me why do ministers shout fire, do they know why? He then continued speaking but that question stuck with me and the Holy Ghost soon gave me the answer. He is the fire!

For our God *is* a consuming fire. (Heb 12:29 KJV)

Love is a fire. Perhaps you have fallen in Love before. Know that here I am speaking of even as a non believer. When someone has a desire or affection for someone else in the Eros (sexual) Love type of way they feel something in them. They feel a fire in them when they see or hear of that person. This is of God.

Even just in an emotional way from the soul there is fire. The soul can generate this kind of Love but it must be of God. If it is affection driven by the wrong force (the devil), it is still a burning but of lust. That is wrong Love and must be quenched. It is counterfeit fire. We dealt with this on day one of this book

.

For by means of a whorish woman *a man is brought* to a piece of bread: and the adulteress will hunt for the precious life. Can a man take fire in his bosom, and his clothes not be burned? Can one go upon hot coals, and his feet not be burned? So he that goeth in to his neighbour's wife; whosoever toucheth her shall not be innocent. (Pro 6:26-29 KJV)

The Lord will not give someone a fire for a married person. That is lust. A result of someone's wrong desires. The same way homosexuality came about. It was a wrong fire.

Because they do this, God has given them over to shameful passions. Even the women pervert the natural use of their sex by unnatural acts. In the same way the men give up natural sexual relations with women and burn with passion for each other. Men do shameful things with each other, and as a result they bring upon themselves the punishment they deserve for their wrongdoing. (Rom 1:26-27 GNB)

But every man is tempted, when he is drawn away of his own lust, and enticed. (Jas 1:14 KJV)

There is the righteous fire. Which is from the Lord, it is not only seen in Eros kind of Love but all Love. I am just using Eros here because it is commonly misunderstood. The ignorant will say they are in Love when they are actually in lust. The fire they feel is of the soul and flesh. However these are natural feelings the Lord put for real Love. Love is a fire. There will be that burning in a person. The Apostle Paul spoke on this.

I say therefore to the unmarried and widows, It is good for them if they abide even as I. But if they cannot contain, let them marry: for it is better to marry than to burn. (1Co 7:8-9 KJV)

Apostle Paul said if one cannot contain themselves and have strong feelings of Love for someone get married. It is a righteous fire. He said don't remain burning but marry. So when two people burn for each other and come together there is a mighty righteous fire of Love. This is God's design. The marriage Love relationship is a shadow of Christ and the Church. It is not only in Eros that there is a fire of Love. John the Baptist baptized with water but Jesus baptizes with the Holy Ghost and fire.

I indeed baptize you with water unto repentance: but he that cometh after me is mightier than I, whose shoes I am not worthy to bear: he shall baptize you with the Holy Ghost, and *with* fire:
(Mat 3:11 KJV)

To be baptized means to be fully submerged. The baptism of Jesus is when someone is fully submerged in Him. That is the baptism of the Holy Ghost, not just to speak in tongues but to be fully immersed in the Holy Ghost. This is like being put in a fire, all the dirt is burned up. The sign of being baptized in the Holy Ghost is someone who walks in Power. Someone who has had an encounter with Jesus, you will know it. They will never be the same as before.

Personally I have felt different kinds of burns on my flesh, fire, an iron, a stove, I've even had electric shocks but the fire of God is different. It is not like torture or some form of pain but you know something is happening to you from the inside out. No wonder the Apostle John fell like a dead man in the presence of God. His Love is that powerful.

And his feet like unto fine brass, as if they burned in a furnace; and his voice as the sound of many waters. And he had in his right hand seven stars: and out of his mouth went a sharp twoedged sword: and his countenance *was* as the sun shineth in his strength. And when I saw him, I fell at his feet as dead. And he laid his right hand upon me, saying unto me, Fear not; I am the first and the last: (Rev 1:15-17 KJV)

The fire of the Love of God surpasses the flesh and the soul it comes from the Spirit. The examples I gave earlier were of a natural way. The Lord has put that in nature for man to understand and relate. However when you truly feel in the Spirit realm the fire of His Love; you will know. A couple of times in my life I have felt the deep infilling of God's Love in me. Remember His Love is His word. God is Love. When I feel spiritually that infilling every time I know whatever happens next I will be watching or listening to the Lord through me, my body and mind have no control.

Then I said, "I will not make mention of Him, Nor speak anymore in His name." But His word was in my heart like a burning fire Shut up in my bones; I was weary of holding it back, And I could not.
(Jer 20:9 NKJV)

Jeremiah the weeping Prophet realized it is impossible to contain the Love of God. A person will feel like exploding!

I was dumb with silence, I held my peace, *even* from good; and my sorrow was stirred. My heart was hot within me, while I was musing the fire burned: *then* spake I with my tongue, (Psa 39:2-3 KJV)

This is why it is impossible to keep the Church of Jesus Christ quiet. Preachers, prophets, singers, saints and all of the Church are filled with the Love of God. It is a fire in them they cannot contain. It must be let out. In the Old Testament sacrifices were burnt by fire. The Israelites had to roast the Passover lamb with fire. Elijah defeated the prophets of Baal when God answered by fire. He was taken to heaven by chariots of fire. Before the throne John saw seven lamps of fire which are the seven Spirits of God. There is so much revelation in the fire of God. Understand that His fire, His Word and His Love are eternal.

The fire shall ever be burning upon the altar; it shall never go out. (Lev 6:13 KJV)

Prayer

Father thank you for your Spirit within me. Keep me fully submerged in your word, your Love and your fire in Jesus name. Amen

Preachers, prophets, singers, saints and all of the Church are filled with the Love of God. It is a fire in them they cannot contain. It must be let out.

Love Is Patient – Day 21

Love is patient, love is kind. It does not envy, it does not boast, it is not proud.
(1Co 13:4 NIV)

The first attribute of Love is patience. How patient are you? How long are you able to wait before you become anxious or annoyed? Love can wait without being angry, irritated or annoyed. God is patient.

The Lord is not slack concerning his promise, as some men count slackness; but is longsuffering to us-ward, not willing that any should perish, but that all should come to repentance. (2Pe 3:9 KJV)

When most people lose patience with sinners and want to see them judged for their sins, God will still wait. He can wait for a very long time for someone to repent. He is slow to anger and it is impossible for Him to make a rash judgment. People who are short tempered are prone to weakness and can make decisions out of anger. When you have Love in you, you will not be hot tempered or make hasty decisions.

He that is slow to anger *is* better than the mighty; and he that ruleth his spirit than he that taketh a city.
(Pro 16:32 KJV)

When you wait you allow hope to work. There is a certain power that is activated when you learn to hold on until the right time. Patience gives the ability for certain processes to take place. It gives chance to other people as one waits their turn. A proud and arrogant person cannot wait for another. Have you ever been in a queue that isn't moving? The most irritable and impatient people begin to make a lot of noise. Pride, anger and impatience are three terrible triplets. Get rid of them. To everything there is a time and a season. When you know this you learn that at times you have to wait.

"Behold, I send the Promise of My Father upon you; but tarry in the city of Jerusalem until you are endued with power from on high." (Luk 24:49 NKJV)

The early church had to wait for the outpouring of the Holy Ghost. They did not have to pray more or fast, they just had to wait. King David was anointed king while Saul was still king. Samuel the prophet was afraid if King Saul heard he had anointed David because Samuel knew what it meant. I'm certain David knew what being anointed king meant. The anointing had left King Saul and was now on David. If David did not have the Love of God in him, he could've as a young man assumed the kingship from Saul before God's time.

Then Samuel took the horn of oil, and anointed him in the midst of his brethren: and the Spirit of the LORD came upon David from that day forward. So Samuel rose up, and went to Ramah. But the Spirit of the LORD departed from Saul, and an evil spirit from the LORD troubled him. (1Sa 16:13-14 KJV)

David loved the Lord and honoured God's ways and His anointed. David saw King Saul as king even when King Saul hunted him. David did not turn to fight King Saul. It was as though David was waiting for King Saul to correct his wrongs. He was extremely patient to the amazement of his men.

Jesus allowed the ministry of John the Baptist to function. He waited until the appointed time for His baptism and ministry to begin. Love knows how to control power that is patience; that is humility. Let the attribute of patience in Love work and you will be blessed.

But let patience have *her* perfect work, that ye may be perfect and entire, wanting nothing. (Jas 1:4 KJV)

As you let patience work there will be no raw or premature fruit in your life. Waiting for the fruit to ripen and the last rains brings out the best fruit. When God tells you to wait, wait.

Therefore be patient, brethren, until the coming of the Lord. See how the farmer waits for the precious fruit of the earth, waiting patiently for it until it receives the early and latter rain. (Jas 5:7 NKJV)

Declaration

I declare that the Love of God is at work in me. I am not rash or hasty. I allow the virtue of patience to work in me in Jesus name. Amen

---

Pride, anger and impatience are three terrible triplets. Get rid of them.

Love Is Kind - Day 22

Love is patient, love is kind. It does not envy, it does not boast, it is not proud.
(1Co 13:4 NIV)

Love is kind. What is kindness? When the bible speaks of God's kindness it more often than not speaks of His loving-kindness. Loving and kindness are always attached. To be kind nevertheless is to be thoughtful and helpful to someone or something else. It is being generous when you don't have to.

The LORD hath appeared of old unto me, *saying,* Yea, I have loved thee with an everlasting love: therefore with lovingkindness have I drawn thee.
(Jer 31:3 KJV)

Kindness and mercy go hand in hand. When someone deserves death but instead of death receives life that is mercy. A person deserves punishment but they get a reward instead.
Mercy is shown and then the goodness of God comes as kindness. The Hebrew word for loving-kindness a number of times is directly translated as mercy. Who are we to show mercy and kindness to?

And he answering said, Thou shalt love the Lord thy God with all thy heart, and with all thy soul, and with all thy strength, and with all thy mind; and thy neighbour as thyself. And he said unto him, Thou hast answered right: this do, and thou shalt live. But he, willing to justify himself, said unto Jesus, And who is my neighbour? (Luk 10:27-29 KJV)

A rich young ruler slyly came to Jesus with a question on what is the greatest commandment. Jesus said Love God and your neighbour as yourself. The young ruler then asked for an explanation as to who was his neighbour. Jesus responded with the story of the Good Samaritan.

A man was robbed on a journey from Jerusalem to Jericho. Historians mention that this was a dangerous journey. The first mentioned was a Priest who saw the wounded man but didn't approach him, the priest walked on. Then a Levite came and looked at the man but also continued. A Samaritan then saw the man, attended to him and paid for his stay at an Inn (hotel). The man most likely was an Israelite. As a Samaritan this was his enemy. The priest and the Levite had positions in society and were expected to help and show kindness.

The Samaritan was the least expected to help the man but he did. This is what Love does it shows mercy and helps. The Samaritan showed kindness to the stranger by spending his time, effort and money on him.

"So which of these three do you think was neighbor to him who fell among the thieves?" And he said, "He who showed mercy on him." Then Jesus said to him, "Go and do likewise." (Luk 10:36-37 NKJV)

It is much easier to be generous to those you know or who you see as close with you such as relatives, countrymen and the like. This Samaritan showed kindness and proved his Love not just to a complete stranger but one who in society was seen as his enemy. This is what God does. He helps strangers and enemies. It is His nature. It is the nature of Love to help even those who some may say don't deserve to be helped. God showed this when He sent His prophet Jonah to warn the people of Nineveh to repent. They were not seen as God's people yet God warned them and had mercy on them.

The generosity of Love does not have payback as a motivator. Love does not help because it wants something in return. The wickedness of the world teaches that there is nothing for free, nobody just helps without a motive. Children of God are children of Love and should be able to help with no strings attached. God does it because it is who He is. We also should because it is who we are. Love is kind.

But love your enemies and be kind and do good [doing favors so that someone derives benefit from them] and lend, expecting and hoping for nothing in return but considering nothing as lost and despairing of no one; and then your recompense (your reward) will be great (rich, strong, intense, and abundant), and you will be sons of the Most High, for He is kind and charitable and good to the ungrateful and the selfish and wicked. (Luk 6:35 AMP)

Act

Be merciful and kind.

> **This is what God does. He helps even strangers and enemies. It is His nature. It is the nature of Love to help even those who some may say don't deserve to be helped.**

Love Does Not Envy – Day 23

Love suffers long and is kind; love does not envy; love does not parade itself, is not puffed up;
(1Co 13:4 NKJV)

Love is patient, kind and does not envy. Jealousy and envy can be put in the same boat here. When there is covetousness; a strong desire for something that is not yours its wrong. This can lead to all kinds of wickedness and is very far from the Love of God. If someone sees someone blessed with something and desires that thing it is wrong. There is no problem if you desire to have the same thing but not the one belonging to another. Let me give a clear example. If your friend has the latest Mercedes Benz you can admire it and get your own of the same make. If however you admire and want the very car your friend has even against his will it's wrong. The car belongs to your friend, envy and jealousy can cause a person to take the car by force.

Please understand the difference between this wicked jealousy and the righteous jealousy in Love. With righteous jealousy a person is protective over what is rightfully theirs. With wicked jealousy a person desires what is not theirs. Joseph's brothers were envious of his dreams.

Then he dreamed still another dream and told it to his brothers, and said, "Look, I have dreamed another dream. And this time, the sun, the moon, and the eleven stars bowed down to me." So he told it to his father and his brothers; and his father rebuked him and said to him, "What is this dream that you have dreamed? Shall your mother and I and your brothers indeed come to bow down to the earth before you?" And his brothers envied him, but his father kept the matter in mind. (Gen 37:9-11 NKJV)

Joseph's family understood that this dream meant he was a ruler over them. Israel his father rebuked Joseph but his brothers envied him. Joseph's father kept the matter meaning he got the message that there was something special about Joseph. At the time though being the father he was trying to keep order as the head. This is why he can be forgiven for his rebuke. His brothers however took the position of envy. They became jealous of his dreams.

A lesson here is don't tell everyone your dreams in particular those who may be jealous of you. An envious person never openly reveals their envy especially to whoever they are envious of. This is the evil of the devil; envy is done in a cunning, secretive, crafty way just like a snake. It waits for an opportunity to strike. There is no envy in Love!

When Joseph's brothers saw him coming, they recognized him in the distance and made plans to kill him. "Here comes that dreamer!" they exclaimed. "Come on, let's kill him and throw him into a deep pit. We can tell our father that a wild animal has eaten him. Then we'll see what becomes of all his dreams!" (Gen 37:18-20 NLT)

Love thinks no evil. Before Joseph came near his brothers had already planned to kill him. All this was just because they didn't like that he was favoured above them. Joseph was given as a blessing to their family and the world. Envy had blinded them all. They did not receive him but questioned why him and not them. Envy is absent of Love and will cause you to fail to receive the blessings God gives. Insecurity in the importance and value of yourself is almost always due to envy of another.

These brothers could not see their own value although Joseph was more valuable. They felt worthless and valueless. That was not true! Levi had the priestly lineage in him the likes of Moses. Judah had been chosen to be a forefather of the very son of God; Jesus Christ! Yet for envy they were blind. Child of God learn to celebrate the gifts in others it cannot remove your own gift! Don't be jealous.

Joseph was received in Egypt. This time all those who had him were not envious of him but welcomed and enjoyed him as a blessing. They wished Joseph well. Goodwill is the opposite of envy. Note Potiphar's wife was not jealous of Joseph but plotted evil against him because Joseph did not agree to her sinful suggestions. Pothiphar, the prison head and Pharaoh all celebrated Joseph's gifts and were not envious or jealous of him. What was the result? All three had their lives made easier and were tremendously blessed. Envy and jealousy is a bitter poison someone swallows. Kick it out!

From then on, because of Joseph the LORD blessed the household of the Egyptian and everything that he had in his house and in his fields. Potiphar turned over everything he had to the care of Joseph and did not concern himself with anything except the food he ate. Joseph was well-built and good-looking, (Gen 39:5-6 GNB)

He put Joseph in charge of all the other prisoners and made him responsible for everything that was done in the prison. The jailer did not have to look after anything for which Joseph was responsible, because the LORD was with Joseph and made him succeed in everything he did. (Gen 39:22-23 GNB)

When the Egyptians began to be hungry, they cried out to the king for food. So he ordered them to go to Joseph and do what he told them. The famine grew worse and spread over the whole country, so Joseph opened all the storehouses and sold grain to the Egyptians. People came to Egypt from all over the world to buy grain from Joseph, because the famine was severe everywhere. (Gen 41:55-57 GNB)

Envy refuses to receive what someone else has, it tries to claim or lower the position of that person at all costs. It does not matter the extent a person goes, envy is envy and must be rooted out. It maybe as a leader you notice God raises someone gifted. In order to keep your position as say the head singer you limit that person's time to sing. It may seem a small thing but it is a root of jealousy, envy and bitterness. It will trouble you not the other person!

God is not the author of confusion. Whoever you reject wrongly you will find yourself like Josephs brothers bowing before Joseph asking for food. Humble yourself admit what someone has is good. It does not mean you do not have anything good. Celebrate the gifts, qualities and achievements of others they are there to bless you and not curse you.

Looking diligently lest any man fail of the grace of God; lest any root of bitterness springing up trouble *you,* and thereby many be defiled; (Heb 12:15 KJV)

Humility is also to acknowledge someone is ahead of you in certain things. Pride refuses to accept what someone else has to say. Jesus was wisdom personified yet He still had time to hear what people said. He did not envy the High Priest or any of the religious leaders above Him. He even told the people to honour them and do what they say not what they do. It is the religious leaders who could not accept Jesus because of envy. They saw how everyone followed Jesus and listened to him. They were jealous of Jesus, they knew He was from God yet they killed him for envy!

There was a man of the Pharisees named Nicodemus, a ruler of the Jews. This man came to Jesus by night and said to Him, "Rabbi, we know that You are a teacher come from God; for no one can do these signs that You do unless God is with him." (Joh 3:1-2 NKJV)

But Pilate answered them, saying, Will ye that I release unto you the King of the Jews? For he knew that the chief priests had delivered him for envy. (Mar 15:9-10 KJV)

Those who saw the hand of God upon the life of Jesus received from Him. Those who were envious of Jesus, could not celebrate Him and therefore were not blessed but cursed. Love does not envy and is not proud. Learn to humble yourself and acknowledge the good in others.

Check if there is any envy in you. It's often driven by fear and insecurity; a fear of being replaced. In the work place, sporting teams, churches and almost every organization. Jealousy and envy prevent a blessing. Are you suppressing someone? Even if it's denying that extra opportunity to sing it can lead to conspiracy to kill later on.

But if ye have bitter envying and strife in your hearts, glory not, and lie not against the truth. This wisdom descendeth not from above, but *is* earthly, sensual, devilish. For where envying and strife *is*, there *is* confusion and every evil work. (Jas 3:14-16 KJV)

Deal with the baby demon before it grows into a monster. Is it a sibling, pastor or coworker who always seems to get the praise? Do you see them as being proud? Maybe you are jealous of them. Uproot jealousy and envy. A way to know you have an issue is to ask the Holy Ghost. A way to overcome it is to celebrate that person and receive them as a blessing. Love wishes goodwill it does not envy.

Prayer

Holy Spirit I want to Love like you do. Show me if I have envy for anyone or anything. Uproot that envy and help me receive and celebrate the grace you have put in my life in particular in people in Jesus name. Amen.

Child of God learn to celebrate the gifts in others it cannot remove your own gift! Don't be jealous.

Love Is Not Proud - Day 24

Love is patient, love is kind. It does not envy, it does not boast, it is not proud.
(1Co 13:4 NIV)

Pride is destructive. The bible tells us pride goes before a fall. Arrogance, boastfulness, self praise and too much attention on oneself is pride. This is different to having pride in what you do. To take pride in yourself and your work is self love which is important. This is when you value and respect yourself and your life. It is having a sense of dignity. The Lord Jesus said Love your neighbour as you Love yourself. When this however is exaggerated that is now being big headed and puffed up. That is no longer self Love it's over stepping the boundaries of pride with dignity and is now sinful pride.

Love never gives up. Love cares more for others than for self. Love doesn't want what it doesn't have. Love doesn't strut, Doesn't have a swelled head,
(1Co 13:4 MSG)

People who are proud usually are the last to find out they have an issue with pride because they hardly listen to people. They are stubborn, argumentative, want the last word and never see themself as wrong. They will always find a way of justifying their actions. With Christians they'll often say God has forgiven me or God said I should do it. Even if the Lord forgave you or told you to do something it does not mean you were right. Just ask the prophet Balaam. (See Numbers 22)

Humility accepts correction pride doesn't. It is how some people leave churches. They don't want to receive correction and believe they are right. For Love to function there must be no pride. How can a father perfect their son if the son is proud and never accepts correction?

Some saints receive discipline but not correction because they are proud. Let me clarify this. Let's say for an example an usher has been found to have problem with flirting. The usher is then spoken to by the pastor and told not to usher for say one month. This usher believes their behaviour was not wrong but nevertheless sits down for one month and adheres to everything the pastor said. This usher will flirt again because they received the disciplinary action but not the correction. Pride prevented the usher's character from being corrected and perfected.

Pride goes before destruction, and a stiff spirit before a fall. (Pro 16:18 BBE)

The children of Israel were hard hearted and stiff necked. They did not want to change their character. This is why they could not inherit what God had for them. Pride prevents you from receiving from God. If you want to work with God there must be no envy and pride in you. Love yourself, love what you do but learn to respect and love others. Most of all respect and take heed to the one's God has put in authority over you whether your leader, boss, parent, teacher or elder. At the same time as a leader respect those under you. It's easier to fall into pride when you are in charge.

**Likewise, ye younger, submit yourselves unto the elder. Yea, all *of you* be subject one to another, and be clothed with humility: for God resisteth the proud, and giveth grace to the humble. (1Pe 5:5 KJV)

God resist the proud! That is a strong statement. To resist means to oppose that is not just to reject but to be against. As in politics you have a ruling party and an opposition party. Or in a sport where two teams are playing against each other. Each team sees the other as an opposition they do not help the opposing team. Pride is in opposition to Love. I'm certain no one wants to be found to be against God. Sadly some believers in Jesus because of pride grieve His Spirit and He is against them.

But they rebelled, and vexed his holy Spirit: therefore he was turned to be their enemy, *and* he fought against them. (Isa 63:10 KJV)

It is possible for a born again Christian to be full of pride and hinder their own life. In this case they are at loggerheads with Love. God desires to restore such a person but they must accept correction. If someone refuses correction and repentance they are proud and will find that God is resisting them. This is why some people can pray, give and do everything but face frustration. If they do not address what the Lord told them to, their many works will not get their prayers answered.

But if ye be without chastisement, whereof all are partakers, then are ye bastards, and not sons. (Heb 12:8 KJV)

Now no chastening for the present seemeth to be joyous, but grievous: nevertheless afterward it yieldeth the peaceable fruit of righteousness unto them which are exercised thereby. (Heb 12:11 KJV)

The chastisement of God is His correction. Only one who humbles themselves can receive His correction. Love corrects and produces the fruit of righteousness which is life.

Hear counsel, and receive instruction, that thou mayest be wise in thy latter end. *There are* **many devices in a man's heart; nevertheless the counsel of the LORD, that shall stand.** (Pro 19:20-21 KJV)

To reverence and respect God is humility. God is Love. Whoever respects and values the qualities and attributes of Love will be humble. By humility and the fear (reverence) of the Lord are riches, honour and life. When you value the word of God you value the things of God. This is humility; seeking the face of God not because you have to, or to prove a point but because you want to. Studying the word of God not because you have to preach or teach but because you want to know more about Jesus. Love does things not to be seen, for itself, neither does Love seek credit for what it does; this is humility.

Pride will always boast, shout and proclaim even the smallest of achievements. Pride always makes mention of self, it is selfish. Love is not selfish but generous. The favour of God comes upon the humble but the proud will fall.

King Nebuchadnezzar was a very interesting character as king of Babylon. His kingdom was mighty in its time. He had the Hebrew wise men to counsel him with God's guidance. The Lord gave the king dreams with messages. One dream warned him that his pride would have him turned mad for some years and live with wild animals. Pride is an enemy of Love. The king in pride did not heed the warning and became like a mad wild animal. Yet thanks to the mercy of God he was restored.

The king thought, "Look how great Babylon is! I built the royal palace by my own impressive power and for my glorious honor." Before the words came out of his mouth, a voice said from heaven, "King Nebuchadnezzar, listen to this: The kingdom has been taken from you. You will be forced away from people and live with the wild animals. You will eat grass like cattle. And seven time periods will pass until you realize that the Most High has power over human kingdoms and that he gives them to whomever he wishes." Just then the prediction about Nebuchadnezzar came true. He was forced away from people and ate grass like cattle. Dew from the sky made his body wet until his hair grew as long as eagles' feathers and his nails grew as long as birds' claws. (Dan 4:30-33 GW)

God resists the proud but gives grace to the humble. Whether for a believer or an unbeliever these spiritual laws still apply. King Herod was killed on the spot by an angel of the Lord because he did not glorify God but like Nebuchadnezzar glorified himself.

On the appointed day Herod, wearing his royal robes, sat on his throne and delivered a public address to the people. They shouted, "This is the voice of a god, not of a man." Immediately, because Herod did not give

praise to God, an angel of the Lord struck him down, and he was eaten by worms and died.
(Act 12:21-23 NIV)

We are dependent on God. No one can boast in themselves but in God. This is humility acknowledging you are what you are by Gods grace. You can do what you can do by God's power. It is His Love and life at work in us. Alone we are nothing.

But he that glorieth, let him glory in the Lord. For not he that commendeth himself is approved, but whom the Lord commendeth. (2Co 10:17-18 KJV)

The boastful and proud praise themselves way too much. The number of times you mention "I" when speaking reveals your level of pride. Reduce the "I's" and rather speak of the Lord and others. Pride they say is like bad breadth, everybody knows who has it but the one with it is always the last to find out. Depend on Jesus He will keep you humble and uplift you.

Let another man praise thee, and not thine own mouth; a stranger, and not thine own lips.
(Pro 27:2 KJV)

Love is humble and does not need to speak of what it does. The power of Love is felt and spoken about widely and cannot be silenced.

Act

Reverence God and stay humble.

Pride always makes mention of self it is selfish. Love is not selfish but generous. The favour of God comes upon the humble but the proud will fall.

Love Is Not Rude – Day 25

Love is not rude, is not selfish, and does not get upset with others. Love does not count up wrongs that have been done. (1Co 13:5 NCV)

One of the primary things instilled in children at an early age is to be well mannered. Any parent with a modest to good upbringing knows it is essential to train children to be mannerly. The behaviour of a young child even a five year old can have a positive or negative reflection on the parents. Schools and businesses alike get a reputation based on the manners of their students and staff. Love is not rude but well mannered and respectful.

Love is not ill-mannered or selfish or irritable; love does not keep a record of wrongs;
(1Co 13:5 GNB)

Being rude reveals the character of a person. Rudeness has good friends, arrogance and pride, both enemies of Love. I recall watching a reality show "The Apprentice". In this show a reputable billionaire was to pick an ideal apprentice to be a part of his team. Some participants were top business people who already had achieved great things with reputations in business. Each episode contestants would compete and then one would be fired till the eventual winner was hired.

In one episode without judging based on tasks a contestant was instantly fired. He was puzzled. The man was one of the highest rated to win the show. He was shown footage of his arrival. He was very rude towards the porter at the hotel. He was told because of his ill treatment of someone who he thought was unimportant he had no place in the organization. The other contestants learnt a great lesson in business right there. It in fact is a life lesson, Love is not rude. Everyone ought to be treated with respect regardless of social standing.

My brothers, as believers in our glorious Lord Jesus Christ, don't show favoritism. Suppose a man comes into your meeting wearing a gold ring and fine clothes, and a poor man in shabby clothes also comes in. If you show special attention to the man wearing fine clothes and say, "Here's a good seat for you," but say to the poor man, "You stand there" or "Sit on the floor by my feet," have you not discriminated among yourselves and become judges with evil thoughts?
(Jas 2:1-4 NIV)

Love is not fake. There is no hypocrisy in Love. Hypocrites are on their best behaviour when a person of influence is watching. "When the cat is away the mice will play". As soon as the leader is away disrespectful subordinates begin to fool around. When the boss is at work everyone is working. When the head pastor is around everyone is serving well. How someone behaves when no one is watching reveals their true character. Love is polite, kind and true not based on eye service.

Children, do the orders of your fathers and mothers in all things, for this is pleasing to the Lord. Fathers, do not be hard on your children, so that their spirit may not be broken. Servants, in all things do the orders of your natural masters; not only when their eyes are on you, as pleasers of men, but with all your heart, fearing the Lord: Whatever you do, do it readily, as to the Lord and not to men;

(Col 3:20-23 BBE)

Be well mannered and respectful for the sake of your Love for the Lord and His Love in you. Anyone who functions by Love will eventually see promotion. A deceiver may deceive people for a while but the Spirit of truth will expose their character in life. Remain humble and truthful don't join the club of men pleasers who seem to be making it in life.

And now we call the proud happy; yea, they that work wickedness are set up; yea, *they that* **tempt God are even delivered. Then they that feared the LORD spake often one to another: and the LORD hearkened, and heard** *it,* **and a book of remembrance was written before him for them that feared the LORD, and that thought upon his name.** (Mal 3:15-16 KJV)

As you hold on to the principles of the Kingdom of God you will be remembered and honoured. Love is not rude. This means Love is respectful and greets. Love does not wait to be greeted but greets. I recall attending a crusade of a famous minister once. I arrived early and He and his team were preparing for the evening event. As the team was setting up whenever one of them saw me they came over and greeted me. I began to walk around and greet them. This changed my life forever. Usually the excuse of busyness is a reason for not greeting. I saw Love in these people. I was not the only early bird there mind you. The team greeted everyone who had come in.

All the brethren greet you. Greet ye one another with an holy kiss. (1Co 16:20 KJV)

Humility greets first! Love greets everyone! I understand in most cultures the younger should approach the Elders first in greeting, rightfully so. However it takes humility to approach someone and greet them. Even if you are older or higher greet those younger or below you. Please get the point here. It is not about trying to greet everyone every time it is about an attitude, which has the intention to greet and show Love to all. The Lord knows your heart. At times the Lord may say go straight to minister don't speak to anyone prior. These are exceptions or if you truly are in the middle of a task.

Greet one another with a kiss of love. Peace to you all who are in Christ Jesus. Amen. (1Pe 5:14 CAB)

Avoidance is a symptom of an issue. When people avoid greeting others they often have something against that person. At times when I notice people avoiding me I rush to greet them first. Love greets! Pride and arrogance gets you nowhere fast. Don't go around saying these people are rude and don't greet. My definition of not greeting is when you greet someone and they ignore you. Don't say they did not come and greet me. Be the first to greet, it's called Love!

Let your speech *be* alway with grace, seasoned with salt, that ye may know how ye ought to answer every man. (Col 4:6 KJV)

Love knows how to speak and address people. The way

in which someone speaks reveals their identity. The use of vulgar language, slander and insults is not the language of the Spirit of God. Certain words must not be in a Christian's vocabulary. Learn how to speak to people without being rude or harsh. Words can build up and destroy. This does not mean you have to be polite with the devil or his agents. Jesus rebuked the wicked and was not rude or sinful when he did it. Being well mannered does not mean you become a softy or a punching bag for all! Just hear the words of Jesus when He spoke about speech.

"Brood of vipers! How can you, being evil, speak good things? For out of the abundance of the heart the mouth speaks. "A good man out of the good treasure of his heart brings forth good things, and an evil man out of the evil treasure brings forth evil things. "But I say to you that for every idle word men may speak, they will give account of it in the day of judgment. "For by your words you will be justified, and by your words you will be condemned."
(Mat 12:34-37 NKJV)

Jesus called these religious leaders snakes. If a baby Christian hears a pastor call another pastor a snake and evil they may say he is being rude and hateful. Yet Jesus did this, He was a religious teacher calling other religious teachers children of the devil and was not wrong or rude. It is important to see all things through the eyes of the Spirit of God. There is a balance; Love is not rude but it does rebuke.

Act

Be respectful and well mannered but not a door mat.

My definition of not greeting is when you greet someone and they ignore you. Don't say they did not come and greet me. Be the first to greet, it's called Love!

There is a balance; Love is not rude but it does rebuke.

Love Is Not Self-Seeking – Day 26

It is not rude, it is not self-seeking, it is not easily angered, it keeps no record of wrongs.
(1Co 13:5 NIV)

Selfishness is a cause of many problems around the world today. People with a fear of missing out try by all means to get. Fear is contrary to Love and produces all forms of wickedness. Insecurity in oneself leads to selfishness. The solution is to follow the word of God! Love is not selfish instead it is selfless. It thinks about others and puts others first.

Look not every man on his own things, but every man also on the things of others. Let this mind be in you, which was also in Christ Jesus: (Php 2:4-5 KJV)

Let this mind be in you. Which mind is that? It is the mind that Jesus had when He was here on earth. He came on earth with a mindset of helping people. Take note there is a difference between being a people pleaser and helping people! Ultimately Jesus had a mindset of pleasing the Father. As He did what Our Heavenly Father asked He helped people.

"For I have come down from heaven, not to do My own will, but the will of Him who sent Me.
(Joh 6:38 NKJV)

God is not selfish. He sent His son on a mission, a mission of sacrificial Love. The plan God had was for His son to prove what His Love is. A selfish person cannot give what is theirs. Stingy people cannot part with money and material things. Why? Money and material things in this world are a measure of value, a measure of someone's effort and labour, their time. Selfless people freely give. Jesus gave His life. Jesus lived a selfless life. We should do likewise.

And *that* he died for all, that they which live should not henceforth live unto themselves, but unto him which died for them, and rose again. (2Co 5:15 KJV)

Live for God and you fulfill the aspect of the selflessness of Love. Selfishness is not concerned about the well being of others. Selfishness is only concerned about itself. Someone who is only interested in their career, their business, their spouse, their children, their car, their schedule and so on has little to no concern for the Lord. Whoever has minimal interest in the things of the Kingdom of God has limited concern for people. Whoever Loves God loves His ways and loves people. Not just in word with lip service but actively with works.

Dear children, let us not love with words or tongue but with actions and in truth. (1Jn 3:18 NIV).

The Apostle Paul declared that he was dead but alive in Christ. Love dies to self will. It starts with the little things. For an example a brother or sister in Christ may ask you to escort them on a short journey. At the very time say you have an exciting event to attend but you don't have to attend. By dying to self you will skip your event and go along with your friend in Christ. It would've been easy to say sorry I'm busy I can't make it. Love costs. I believe this is why the Lord uses money and material wealth as a quality test.

He that is faithful in that which is least is faithful also in much: and he that is unjust in the least is unjust also in much. If therefore ye have not been faithful in the unrighteous mammon, who will commit to your trust the true *riches?* (Luk 16:10-11 KJV)

Arguments are always given that the ones who give have the ability to give. The truth reveals that some of the most selfish people in the world are poor people. Everyone has something to give. In the bible we see a poor widow giving everything! Love is generous and gives. A rich person gives by employing people. A poor person cannot even allow an investor in their tiny business because they think the investor wants their money!

Give, and it shall be given unto you; good measure, pressed down, and shaken together, and running over, shall men give into your bosom. For with the same measure that ye mete withal it shall be measured to you again. (Luk 6:38 KJV)

As you study the gospels the Holy Spirit will reveal to you many things. For instance in the ministry of Jesus what is mentioned matters. There were many other events but we are told what was recorded is what was more essential. Recall when there were multitudes of hungry people. We are told there was a boy with five loaves of bread and two fish. Why? This boy offered his lunch for the people. He must have given it to the disciples to distribute. How often a call to give is made and few respond to the call? Many people have but not all are willing to give. Why? Selfishness, people look to someone else to do something. The "someone else" will be blessed. In this case I'm certain the twelve baskets left over were given to the boy. The Lord looks at situations across the world and marvels that no one will rise to deal with a situation. This is why He had to come and redeem us.

I looked, but there was no one to help, And I wondered That there was no one to uphold; Therefore My own arm brought salvation for Me; And My own fury, it sustained Me. (Isa 63:5 NKJV)

Love is considerate. The Lord is looking for that person who will say this situation needs help, Lord use me to solve this problem. The selfish continue with their lives. When you dedicate your life to people as led by God you will actually live life and discover your purpose. Those who seek their own things miss it. A person who is ever trying to build their career, their family, their name, without helping anyone will lose their life. Live led by Love and realize life.

Those who want to save their lives will lose them. But those who lose their lives for me will find them.
(Mat 16:25 GW)

Act

Live a selfless life. Live for Jesus and be blessed!

Live for God and you fulfill the aspect of the selflessness of Love.

Love Is Not Easily Provoked – Day 27

Does not behave indecently, does not seek her own, is not easily provoked, thinks no evil.
(1Co 13:5 MKJV)

Love is patient, kind, does not envy, is not proud and is not rude. Love is selfless and not easily provoked. What does it mean to be easily provoked? Have you ever known someone who snaps at anything? Someone who is short tempered and easily offended? People can blame genes and say well their mother, father or whosoever also had a short temper; it runs in the family. This does not apply to a child of God. Neither does it apply to anyone who chooses to walk in Love. Love is not short tempered.

It is not rude, it is not self-seeking, it is not easily angered, it keeps no record of wrongs.
(1Co 13:5 NIV)

Anyone who has Love working in them is not easily angered. The excuse of people who say they are; "like that", is a refusal to change. In particular for born again Christians; never believe the lie that says it is how you are or how that person is. When you come to Christ you are made new.

Therefore if any man *be* **in Christ,** *he is* **a new creature: old things are passed away; behold, all things are become new. (2Co 5:17 KJV)**

If you have had anger issues it means you have Love

issues. Anyone who allows Love to work is not easily angry or offended. Children of God are born of Love but must choose to obey Love. It is not a sin to be angry but it is a sin to hold anger or react out of human anger. God is not short tempered. Have a look at His patience with the nation of Israel. Not just from the exodus out of Egypt but even all their idolatry later. The Lord still redeemed them. He did become angry but after a lot of betrayal and provoking from Israel.

How oft did they provoke him in the wilderness, *and* **grieve him in the desert! Yea, they turned back and tempted God, and limited the Holy One of Israel. They remembered not his hand,** *nor* **the day when he delivered them from the enemy.**
(Psa 78:40-42 KJV)

To have a heart seeking God is to have a desire for Love. From here someone's character is perfected. To be easily angered is a weak character. To be used by the Lord is to be used by Love. This means regardless of the wrong done against you, you are not quick to become angry or to react with human anger. The character of Jesus in the gospels gives us our best representation of Love in action. Jesus was always under accusation from the religious devils. Yet he remained calm and always answered with the wisdom of God. If someone is easily angered they can blurt out words and do things they never intended.

Dealing with short tempered people is dealing with people insensitive to Love. This is the truth of the Word of God. All scripture is given by inspiration of God and is profitable for teaching and instruction. Anyone who welcomes and follows Love will not be easily provoked. It is so difficult to work with short tempered people. It is like walking on a thin glass floor; it can easily crack even though you tread cautiously. The solution is submission to the Spirit of God. Love is slow to anger and not easily provoked.

As a child of God you must realize not everything requires a response or reaction. Provocation is there to get a person to fight. Why waste your breath to respond to untrue insults? Why waste your energy to react to insults?

Answer not a fool according to his folly, lest thou also be like unto him. (Pro 26:4 KJV)

Do not let the devil provoke you. He may use anyone or anything just to make you angry. Love does not become angry easily. If you do become angry do not react or keep the anger. Keeping anger is more dangerous than reacting in anger. Keeping anger is when a person remains silent but inside is upset. This is where anger gets turned into bitterness and after a long time the person explodes like a volcano.

Be ye angry, and sin not: let not the sun go down upon your wrath: Neither give place to the devil. (Eph 4:26-27 KJV)

To react angrily or to hold anger will allow the devil to work. In this case God is absent. If you get angry it's not a sin but what you do with the anger is what matters. There is righteous anger which brings about a reaction which is not sin. We see this when Jesus chased the money changers out of the Temple.

Here is some advice, if ever you find yourself angry in a situation. Flee the scene and cool down before you react. This is personal advice. Pray and ask the Lord to calm you down and respond righteously. The enemy wants you weak. When you are provoked human anger can takeover. Let the Holy Spirit remain in control. He will guide you on what to do next or if at all you should do anything. Importantly don't hold anger and offense. These things are not in unity with the Spirit of God.

He who is slow to anger is better than the mighty, and he who rules his spirit is better than he who takes a city. (Pro 16:32 MKJV)

Being slow to anger is an attribute of God. It is also a sign of His mercy. Remember the first thing that Love is, is patient. A patient person is not short tempered or easily provoked. It is power to be able to control yourself. Love is not reckless but can control itself. You will be patient and merciful as you submit to the Lord.

Act

Let Love work in you. Rule your spirit and be not easily angered.

Love is slow to anger and not easily provoked.

Love Thinks No evil – Day 28

Love suffers long and is kind; love does not envy; love does not parade itself, is not puffed up; does not behave rudely, does not seek its own, is not provoked, thinks no evil; (1Co 13:4-5 NKJV)

Love does not think any evil. As it is impossible for God to lie so it is impossible for Him to think evil. In light there is only goodness and righteousness whereas darkness is full of evil and unrighteousness. God is light.

Every good gift and every perfect gift is from above, and cometh down from the Father of lights, with whom is no variableness, neither shadow of turning. (Jas 1:17 KJV)

God is Love and is opposite to fear and evil. He does not use evil in any way for anything. He cannot even think evil because He is righteous. God cannot be tempted with evil or weakened by it. This means Love cannot be tempted by evil or weakened by evil. When you allow Love to work in and through you, you will not be affected by evil.

Let no one say when he is tempted, I am tempted from God; for God is incapable of being tempted by [what is] evil and He Himself tempts no one. (Jas 1:13 AMP)

Understand that any evil thing that comes upon someone is not the plan or thought of God. God does not think evil towards people; everything He does is righteous and right. He does not make mistakes. He is perfect, Love is perfect. Accidents, tragedies, sickness, disease and the like are not God's plan. No sane person would ever wish such on someone they dearly Love. Jesus revealed how much God loves us when He spoke of evil parents answering children's requests.

"Suppose your children ask for bread. Which of you will give them a stone? Or suppose your children ask for a fish. Which of you will give them a snake? Even though you are evil, you know how to give good gifts to your children. How much more will your Father who is in heaven give good gifts to those who ask him! (Mat 7:9-11 NIRV)

The bible reveals that the heart of someone is who they truly are in their spirit. As someone thinks in their heart is how they are. From the abundance of the heart someone speaks. The words people speak then determine their action. Everything starts from the spirit, the thoughts of the heart. An evil person can pretend but what is truly in their heart?

Do not eat the bread of him who has **an evil eye, nor desire his dainty foods; for as he thinks in his heart, so is he; Eat and drink, he says to you, but his heart is not with you. Your bit** which **you have eaten, you shall vomit up, and spoil your pleasant words.**
(Pro 23:6-8 MKJV)

Love does not pretend to be what it's not. The thoughts of Love are always matched with righteous words and actions. Fruits will always determine good and evil. One of the psalms brings wonderful words about the Lord. These words came about from the heart of the writer thinking good and not evil.

My heart overflows with a good matter. I speak the things which I have made concerning the king. My tongue is the pen of a ready writer.
(Psa 45:1 ACV)

Jesus said from a full heart people speak. When your heart is filled with goodness, wonderful words will come from you. These are words driven by Love. This is how amazing praises and worship come. They come when a Christian thinks about God, thinks about Love, thinks about goodness and right things.

For I know the thoughts that I think toward you, says the LORD, thoughts of peace and not of evil, to give you a future and a hope. (Jer 29:11 NKJV)

The Lord thinks good thoughts and plans good things especially for His children! Love never thinks evil or uses evil. However God can turn the evil from the devil for your good. He is always thinking something good. Like how Joseph was sold because of the evil thoughts of his jealous brothers. God then turned those evil thoughts to work for good for Joseph. God is a master at turning evil into good!

Then his brothers went, and falling at his feet, said, Truly, we are your servants. And Joseph said, Have no fear: am I in the place of God? As for you, it was in your mind to do me evil, but God has given a happy outcome, the salvation of numbers of people, as you see today. (Gen 50:18-20 BBE)

The wonderful Agape Love of God was at work in Joseph all along. Joseph could have done whatever he wished to his brothers. His brothers were afraid when their father (Israel) died. They thought Joseph was pretending to Love them till their father died. They thought Joseph had a hidden agenda with evil thoughts. The only agenda of Love is goodness and affection.

They realized Joseph genuinely loved them, forgave them and cared for them despite the evil they did to him. Joseph told them God turned their evil plan around for good. Love only thinks good things. God is planning good things for you always.

And we know that all things work together for good to them that love God, to them who are the called according to *his* purpose. (Rom 8:28 KJV)

Love keeps no record of wrong. If Joseph did not choose to walk in Love he would've remembered his brother's sins. Joseph treated his brothers as though they never did any evil to him. This is what Love does; it forgets the bad and remembers the good. After you've repented of your sins, you may remember them but Love doesn't. God doesn't remember them, not He doesn't mention them; He doesn't remember them.

Then he adds, "I will never again remember their sins and lawless deeds." (Heb 10:17 NLT)

The blood of Jesus washes away sins. Christians should do as the Lord does especially when someone has repented of their mistakes. Forgive and forget. Love chooses to forgive and forget. If you say you forgave someone but keep reminding them of their sin you haven't truly forgiven them. You have marked that person for their fault. This is what brings rifts in relationships; record keeping of sins. Love thinks no evil it keeps no record of wrong.

It is not rude, it is not self-seeking, it is not easily angered, it keeps no record of wrongs.
(1Co 13:5 NIV)

Act
Think no evil and forgive and forget.

The only agenda of Love is goodness and affection.

This is what Love does; it forgets the bad and remembers the good.

Love Does Not Rejoice In Iniquity - Day 29

It does not rejoice at injustice and unrighteousness, but rejoices when right and truth prevail.
(1Co 13:6 AMP)

Iniquity is injustice and unrighteousness which are all sin. Love does not celebrate iniquity. When there is any wrong doing God is not happy about it. The book of Proverbs highlights specific sins the Lord hates.

These six *things* doth the LORD hate: yea, seven *are* an abomination unto him: A proud look, a lying tongue, and hands that shed innocent blood, An heart that deviseth wicked imaginations, feet that be swift in running to mischief, A false witness *that* speaketh lies, and he that soweth discord among brethren.
(Pro 6:16-19 KJV)

All of the above pride, lying, murder, wicked plans, mischief, false witnessing and an architect of discord among brethren are against Love. God who is Love is against all forms of iniquity. He is against sin. This is what led to the flood during Noah's time and the destruction of Sodom and Gomorrah during Abraham's time. The Lord cannot even look at iniquity.

You are of purer eyes than to behold evil, and can not look on iniquity: (Hab 1:13a KJ2000)

This is why Jesus Christ cried out on the cross as being forsaken. He cried out because He knew the eyes of God had left Him. God does not delight in iniquity. At that point in time Jesus Christ became sin on the cross. The Lord could not look at that because of His holiness.

And at the ninth hour Jesus cried with a loud voice, saying, Eloi, Eloi, lama sabachthani? which is, being interpreted, My God, my God, why hast thou forsaken me? (Mar 15:34 KJV)

This is why as a child of God you should not look at wicked things. In this day people share pictures and videos of tragedies and sinful things. As a child of God you are not to look at such things. Neither should you celebrate when something wicked happens even to a bad person. Love does not delight in wickedness.

"Say to them: 'As I live,' says the Lord GOD, 'I have no pleasure in the death of the wicked, but that the wicked turn from his way and live. Turn, turn from your evil ways! For why should you die, O house of Israel?' (Eze 33:11 NKJV)

Love desires life and truth. Where there is sin it brings forth death. Love is about righteousness and life.

For thou *art* not a God that hath pleasure in wickedness: neither shall evil dwell with thee. (Psa 5:4 KJV)

As a child of God you must celebrate life and not death. Love does not expose sins of people or rejoice in their downfall. Love desires for salvation. The blood of Jesus was shed so that we can come boldly to the Lord. Love rejoices in good news not bad news. Just because something happened does not mean you have to jump on the band wagon and become a bearer of bad news. Gossip and slander should not be shared by children of God. Love does not repeat the mistakes or sins of someone but covers them.

(Re-Read day 8; Love covers a multitude of sins to get better understanding on this)

And above all things have fervent love for one another, for "love will cover a multitude of sins." (1Pe 4:8 NKJV)

Act

Choose not to celebrate sin or spread or look at anything sinful.

Love rejoices in good news not bad news.

Love Rejoices In The Truth ~ Day 30

Rejoiceth not in iniquity, but rejoiceth in the truth;
(1Co 13:6 KJV)

The tenth attribute of Love is that Love rejoices in the truth. As we saw the previous day Love does not rejoice in iniquity but in the truth. What is the truth? Truth is the reality of all things. Truth confirms itself and does not need any defense or to be proved. The truth will always come out in the end. A lie is contrary to truth, it is false and simply put a lie is sin. Lies are false claims of reality in all things.

Jesus saith unto him, I am the way, the truth, and the life: no man cometh unto the Father, but by me.
(Joh 14:6 KJV)

There is only one famous leader to my knowledge who boldly said they are the truth; Jesus of Nazareth. Love celebrates the truth, it celebrates Jesus. Everything Jesus did and said gives us revelation of truth. As a child of Love you ought to spread truth. Truth, righteousness and life go hand in hand. These three function together with Love. The truth needs no defense. The truth is the answer to all wrong. Whenever there is a problem the answer is the truth. Some people fear the truth because they expect to be judged and condemned. The wonderful thing about Love is that wherever truth is there is mercy!

Mercy and truth are met together; righteousness and peace have kissed *each other.* (Psa 85:10 KJV)

The enemy is the source of all lies and wants them to be spread. Lies such as "the truth hurts" have been spread abroad. The truth beloved, only hurts a lie, it hurts the devil. Remain on the side of God who is kind and merciful, stand for the truth and you will not be hurt. Anyone who celebrates and stands for lies without repentance will fall.

Why do ye not understand my speech? *even* because ye cannot hear my word. Ye are of *your* father the devil, and the lusts of your father ye will do. He was a murderer from the beginning, and abode not in the truth, because there is no truth in him. When he speaketh a lie, he speaketh of his own: for he is a liar, and the father of it. (Joh 8:43-44 KJV)

Jesus told this group of people they could not accept His word because it was truth and they were opposed to truth. He told them spiritually they were children of the devil. Truth and lies will never agree. Unless a person repents and accepts the truth they remain bound with evil,

Lies are deceptive. They try to prove themselves with the backing of more lies. In the world today as it was before the enemy publishes lies in mass to get society to accept it as truth. He does the same even in the church. Jesus is the truth eternally. His words and actions as seen in the bible are our standard for life. The word of God is true and will remain true. Check everything through the light of God's word to verify truth. The Spirit of God in you will always confirm the word of God.

By mercy and truth iniquity is purged: and by the fear of the LORD men depart from evil.
(Pro 16:6 KJV)

Love does not rejoice in unrighteousness and lies but in righteousness and truth. The answer to sin is the truth. Jesus paid for all sins and made a relationship with God possible by grace and mercy. Reverence God and spread good news only. Check what you share through truth first regardless of how funny, trending or entertaining something might be. Ask yourself is this thing celebrated by God, does it glorify God. The Lord has the real funny and entertaining stuff. Don't be deceived into publishing or celebrating unrighteousness.

It does not rejoice at injustice and unrighteousness, but rejoices when right and truth prevail.
(1Co 13:6 AMP)

The majority of mainstream media seek to spread bad news, anything disastrous and controversial. It can lead someone to believe there is nothing good in this world. Yet there are many good things taking place. It is up to us as beloved children of God to celebrate righteousness and truth. Share inspiring and encouraging news. Use your platform to publish good news if you are a journalist or in media. The light of God and Glory of God will always shine on what is true.

But all things that are exposed are made manifest by the light, for whatever makes manifest is light.
(Eph 5:13 NKJV)

Act

Choose to celebrate and spread truthful and life giving things.

The truth needs no defense. The truth is the answer to all wrong.

Lies such as "the truth hurts" have been spread abroad. The truth beloved, only hurts a lie, it hurts the devil.

Love Bears All Things - Day 31

Bears all things, believes all things, hopes all things, endures all things. (1Co 13:7 NKJV)

Remember when we began this book the different types of Love were explained. The Love we have been speaking of is the unconditional Love of God (Agape). Love bears all things. This must be understood in context. Let's check the meaning of the word translated as bears in the theme verse above.

G4722

στέγω

stegō

steg'-o

From G4721; to *roof* over, that is, (figuratively) to *cover* with silence (*endure* patiently): - (for-) bear, suffer.

Re; Strong's Dictionary

In the Greek it is a word which means to put a roof on something, as with thatching or other roofing material. Love covers, silences, endures all things. Jesus gave a great explanation of those who hear and do what He says. He likened such people to a house built on a rock.

When a violent storm comes, the house will remain standing because it is built on the rock.

"Therefore whoever hears these sayings of Mine, and does them, I will liken him to a wise man who built his house on the rock: "and the rain descended, the floods came, and the winds blew and beat on that house; and it did not fall, for it was founded on the rock.
(Mat 7:24-25 NKJV)

We have a covering as children of God. The Love of God is our roof that shelters us from every kind of storm. We therefore must choose Love. By choosing Love we choose to be a roof over our neighbour without reason or expectations. The "all things" Love bears with must be understood in this context. Love is able to remain despite someone's numerous mistakes and failures. In this sense we can say the roof we put over someone will not be removed. Natural "Love" and wrong "Love" removes this roof for a reason or when a condition isn't fulfilled.

Forbearance is also the ability to remain silent and hold back when you can rightful take action and withdraw your care. If somebody does evil to you, your ability to still care for them is only possible by Love.

Forbearing one another, and forgiving one another, if any man have a quarrel against any: even as Christ forgave you, so also *do* ye.
(Col 3:13 KJV)

If it were not for the Love of God many people would be kicked out from under His covering. The mercy of God is at work in bearing all things. Many people have escaped death because of the protection of God. This protection is God keeping them under the roof of His Love.

He that dwelleth in the secret place of the most High shall abide under the shadow of the Almighty.
(Psa 91:1 KJV)

In the Old Testament, the Ark of the Covenant had a mercy seat that was covered by the wings of two Cherubim. This is where God said He would meet Moses, a place of Love and protection.

In this world there are certain levels of protection given to people. Presidents, diplomats and billionaires for an example have special high level security. This security is given to them because of who they are. There are conditions and reasons. The security team is trained to put their lives on the line for the one they are protecting. Jesus said that laying down your life for your friend is the greatest act of Love. In this case the security team will be doing their job. In this job however they could just end up performing the greatest act of Love! These protected people are not guaranteed this protection forever. If they lose their status the protection is lifted. Not so with God, His Love remains regardless of all things!

He brought me to the banqueting house, and his banner over me *was* love.
(Son 2:4 KJV)

There is a roof that will not move over our lives. It is the Love of God. This is not just to born again believers but all of mankind whether they believe or not. The Love of God is at work in their lives, including the unthankful and evil. Love bears with the ignorance or opposition of those in the world.

For God so loved the world, that he gave his only begotten Son, that whosoever believeth in him should not perish, but have everlasting life. (Joh 3:16 KJV)

This attribute of Love was seen in the Apostles. Many times Apostle Paul chose to bear with people because of the Love he had for them. A person without the Love of God would have quickly lost patience and left people to die in their sins. Paul did not do this. There are different situations in the word of God where Christians put their lives on the line for the sake of Love. They let things go so the gospel could keep moving.

If we have sown unto you spiritual things, *is it* a great thing if we shall reap your carnal things? If others be partakers of *this* power over you, *are* not we rather? Nevertheless we have not used this power; but suffer all things, lest we should hinder the gospel of Christ. (1Co 9:11-12 KJV)

The Apostle Paul was a tent maker and in some places would work to provide for his needs and still spend his time and money to travel and preach. He was forbearing against the stinginess of those people by sharing the Gospel with Love to them. He did not hold back in correction because Love corrects. He explained to the people that they were meant to partner with him. However he put this aside and continued in Love. Jesus dealt with a lot but did not quit. What are you willing to bear with? Love always forbears, covers and protects.

Bear ye one another's burdens, and so fulfil the law of Christ. (Gal 6:2 KJV)

Act

Follow the example of Paul and bear with people so that God's Love may prevail through you.

We have a covering as children of God. The Love of God is our roof that shelters us from every kind of storm.

Love Believes All Things – Day 32

Love bears all things, believes all things, hopes all things, endures all things. (1Co 13:7 CENT)

Have you ever lost confidence in a person? You may have stood by someone, supported them, forgiven them and continually trusted them to change. Then the person doesn't change from their error. Natural Love will lose patience and faith in such a person. Love however never loses patience or writes someone off. God always trusts that someone can change. Love never doubts a person can repent.

The Lord is not slow in keeping his word, as he seems to some, but he is waiting in mercy for you, not desiring the destruction of any, but that all may be turned from their evil ways. (2Pe 3:9 BBE)

The Lord's bowels of mercy and compassion cause Him to believe someone can repent. Love gives chance after chance to a sinner. Love always believes the best about someone.

Love bears up under anything and everything that comes, is ever ready to believe the best of every person, its hopes are fadeless under all circumstances, and it endures everything [without weakening]. (1Co 13:7 AMP)

Love believes all things. It must be clearly understood here, that "all things" refers to the things of God. Love has the God kind of faith. This is unfailing faith. It is impossible for Love to doubt the things of God. Love is unshakeable in trusting in the Lord. Thus Love makes all things possible and never fails.

And Jesus, answering, said to them, Have God's faith. Truly I say to you, Whoever says to this mountain, Be taken up and be put into the sea; and has no doubt in his heart, but has faith that what he says will come about, he will have his desire. For this reason I say to you, Whatever you make a request for in prayer, have faith that it has been given to you, and you will have it. (Mar 11:22-24 BBE)

There is absolutely no unbelief in Love. Perfect faith is found in Love. God's faith is seen in the life of Jesus of Nazareth, whatever He said and believed happened.

For when we are in union with Christ Jesus, neither circumcision nor the lack of it makes any difference at all; what matters is faith that works through love. (Gal 5:6 GNB)

Confession

I confess that I have received the gift of faith. This faith is at work in me through the perfect Love of God. In Jesus name. Amen

---

There is absolutely no unbelief in Love. Perfect faith is found in Love.

Love Hopes All Things – Day 33

Love bears all things, believes all things, hopes all things, endures all things. (1Co 13:7 CENT)

Once again "all things" here is speaking of the things of God. Love hopes all things in line with the truth of God. Hope is an anchor and a divine connection for great expectations of the future. Love holds on always for the plans of God to be fulfilled. Faith needs to have something to hope for. The Lord's promise for the future is our hope.

And hope maketh not ashamed; because the love of God is shed abroad in our hearts by the Holy Ghost which is given unto us. (Rom 5:5 KJV)

The word of God has made many declarations concerning the children of God. You are the light of the world, you will heal the sick, raise the dead, lend to nations are some of these declarations. If you have not yet seen the fulfillment of these and other declarations you are holding on in hope to see their manifestation. Faith is what will enable you to receive and experience these declarations about you as a child of God. Overall it is Love that empowers us always to hope and receive what God says to us.

And Jesus looking upon them saith, With men *it is* impossible, but not with God: for with God all things are possible. (Mar 10:27 KJV)

Love trusts that all things can happen. There is nothing impossible with God. To lose hope is to say that something is not possible. Circumstances can become so bad that people lose hope. They see it as an irrecoverable, dead situation. With Love there is always hope. Jesus proved this many times during His ministry here on earth.

While He was still speaking, there came some from the ruler's house, who said [to Jairus], Your daughter has died. Why bother and distress the Teacher any further? (Mar 5:35 AMP)

This man Jairus had hope that his daughter would recover from her sickness. He requested Jesus to come and heal her but she died before Jesus arrived. Jairus's servants lost hope; they told Jairus to let Jesus go on, they had no more hope. Jesus who is Love always has hope. Have a look at His response when He heard these servants.

Overhearing but ignoring what they said, Jesus said to the ruler of the synagogue, Do not be seized with alarm and struck with fear; only keep on believing. (Mar 5:36 AMP)

Jesus went on to raise this girl from the dead. Hope makes it possible to keep on believing. Love will always believe something good can come out of a situation. Normal people may say this person has strayed too far from the Lord, there's no hope for them now, but God will still have hope. Whatever the case might be Love still hopes and believes something good is possible.

Keep on believing. With God all things are possible.

Declaration

I declare that all things are possible with God. The Love of God enables me to keep on believing no matter how dark a situation looks. In Jesus name. Amen

For more on Hope read Forty days On Hope By Jason Pullen

Overall it is Love that empowers us always to hope and receive what God says to us.

Love Endures All Things – Day 34

Love bears all things, believes all things, hopes all things, endures all things. (1Co 13:7 CENT)

Endurance is the ability to withstand hardship and adversary. It is staying power. In athletics there are marathon runners. These athletes have to have great stamina to run for hours at times day and night. They experience different kinds of weather and terrain. Soldiers also need great endurance. They have to handle separation from family, loss of their friends in battle, torture from the enemy if captured and worse. Soldiers sign up to die for a cause. Greater Love has no man than to lay down his life for his friends! True soldiers have incredible staying power. As Christians we have the ability to endure.

Take, my brethren, the prophets, who have spoken in the name of the Lord, for an example of suffering affliction, and of patience. Behold, we count them happy which endure. Ye have heard of the patience of Job, and have seen the end of the Lord; that the Lord is very pitiful, and of tender mercy.
(Jas 5:10-11 KJV)

Many of the Prophets in the Old Testament had to handle different types of opposition. At times the one they were sent to deliver a message to from the Lord had them beaten or thrown in prison. Yet they did not quit. Love has staying power; it does not quit. Job went through tremendous affliction, he was a hardcore legend. Many others would've thrown in the towel but Job did not. His friends and wife did not encourage him to endure but he still did. Moses had to be patient and chose to keep his position as leader of the rebellious children of Israel. People who tried to kill him, yet because of the Love and mercy of God Moses held on. As children of God, born of Love we have this power available to us. A never surrender attitude, we should allow it to work.

In which I put up with the hardest conditions, even prison chains, like one who has done a crime; but the word of God is not in chains. (2Ti 2:9 BBE)

The Apostle Paul withstood various trials including prison for the sake of the Gospel of Jesus Christ.

Therefore I endure all things for the elect's sakes, that they may also obtain the salvation which is in Christ Jesus with eternal glory. *It is* **a faithful saying: For if we be dead with** *him,* **we shall also live with** *him:* **If we suffer, we shall also reign with** *him:* **if we deny** *him,* **he also will deny us: If we believe not,** *yet* **he abideth faithful: he cannot deny himself.** (2Ti 2:10-13 KJV)

Paul gave the revelation and reason for suffering for the sake of the Lord. There is the reward of reigning in glory for those who choose to endure for the Lord. I say choose because it is a choice. Some people slow down or stop doing the work of the Lord by choice. They become mediocre or resign from roles in ministry because of hardship, persecution and trials. Beloved there is a reward for those who choose to endure.

Now if we are children, then we are heirs--heirs of

God and co-heirs with Christ, if indeed we share in his sufferings in order that we may also share in his glory. (Rom 8:17 NIV)

Love can endure all things. There is an end to all trials, persecution and hardship Saints may go through for the Lord. The power of His Love in us gives us the staying power and ability to overcome.

You have been put to no test but such as is common to man: and God is true, who will not let any test come on you which you are not able to undergo; but he will make with the test a way out of it, so that you may be able to go through it. (1Co 10:13 BBE)

You are born to win and overcome all things. Love can handle the rough road and keeps on even when the going gets tough. Jesus is the best example of the enduring power of Love. He endured persecution from the ones He came to save. He held on and died for them.

Looking unto Jesus the author and finisher of *our* faith; who for the joy that was set before him endured the cross, despising the shame, and is set down at the right hand of the throne of God. For consider him that endured such contradiction of sinners against himself, lest ye be wearied and faint in your minds. Ye have not yet resisted unto blood, striving against sin. (Heb 12:2-4 KJV)

Act

Choose to endure what the Lord wants you to endure.

Some people slow down or stop doing the work of the Lord by choice. They become mediocre or resign from roles in ministry because of hardship, persecution and trials. Beloved there is a reward for those who choose to endure.

Love Never Fails – Day 35

Love never fails. But whether there are **prophecies, they will fail; whether** there are **tongues, they will cease; whether** there is **knowledge, it will vanish away.**
(1Co 13:8 NKJV)

This is the fifteenth and final attribute of Love given in this revelation in first Corinthians; Love never fails.

The blueprint for a life of excellence without any failure is a sinless life, the life of Jesus of Nazareth. There is never a point we see Jesus failing or making a mistake and repenting. This is because Jesus of Nazareth came to this earth as God in flesh. God is Love and Love never fails. It is impossible for God to fail.

And Jesus looking upon them saith, With men *it is* **impossible, but not with God: for with God all things are possible.** (Mar 10:27 KJV)

This is the truth that all things are made possible by Love. Whenever someone see's something as impossible it's seen as a target that can't be reached; that is failure. The bible declares that with God every target can be reached. For anyone to win in life and not fail, Love is a key ingredient. As Jesus is also the chief cornerstone meaning, He is the most important part of the building. Love is that cornerstone for victory in all things. When you put Love in any situation, the Lord is working with you. With God on your side you cannot fail.

Faithful *is* **he that calleth you, who also will do** *it.*
(1Th 5:24 KJV)

The heroes of faith in the book of Hebrews all had Love as their fuel. They were victorious because their actions were motivated and maintained by Love. Love gives eternal victory.

Love never fails. But where there are prophecies, they will cease; where there are tongues, they will be stilled; where there is knowledge, it will pass away. (1Co 13:8 NIV)

As powerful as prophecies, tongues and knowledge are they can fail at a certain time. This is why to trust in Love which is to trust in God keeps you on the winning side. When you are faced with an insurmountable problem or just day to day challenges you can bank on the Lord. By doing this you are banking on Love. I believe it is not a coincidence that in the translation of the bible into English the absolute central verse in the entire bible is the one below.

It is **better to trust in the LORD than to put confidence in man.** (Psa 118:8 KJV)

Anything outside of the Lord we cannot have confidence in because it can fail. In our relationship with the Lord we must humble ourselves and realize that it is impossible for Him to ever be wrong. He cannot fail therefore He cannot be at fault. Any errors in our life are either an attack of the devil or an error on our part. The notion that God allowed that thing to happen is often ignorance. We can never blame God. Read through the response of the Lord in the book of Job. From that conversation you can fathom the greatness of the Wisdom, power and excellence of the Lord.

Then the LORD answered Job out of the whirlwind, and said: "Who is this who darkens counsel By words without knowledge? Now prepare yourself like a man; I will question you, and you shall answer Me. "Where were you when I laid the foundations of the earth? Tell Me, if you have understanding. Who determined its measurements? Surely you know! Or who stretched the line upon it? To what were its foundations fastened? Or who laid its cornerstone, (Job 38:1-6 NKJV)

This is just an extract above. The depths of the Lord cannot be searched out. This is why the book of revelation reveals non-stop worship. That is because the excellence of God is endless. When you choose to be on the side of God you are on the side of Love; there is no failure there. Light exists in darkness but darkness cannot exist in light. This is the clearest declaration using natural phenomena that God always triumphs over failure and evil.

The light shines through the darkness, and the darkness can never extinguish it. (Joh 1:5 NLT)

Declaration

I declare that I choose the winning side. I choose Love. I choose Jesus Christ. I choose to be led by Love and win in all situations in Jesus name. Amen

---

Light exists in darkness but darkness cannot exist in light. This is the clearest declaration using natural phenomena that God always triumphs over failure and evil.

Love Versus Fear - Day 36

There is no fear in love; but perfect love casteth out fear: because fear hath torment. He that feareth is not made perfect in love. (1Jn 4:18 KJV)

By now your understanding of what Love is should be deeper. Earlier on in this book we saw that to hate is also seen as to love less (see day.9). The opposite of Love however is not hate but fear. This truth is shown in our opening verse. There is no fear in Love but perfect Love casts out fear. As you ought to understand by now perfect Love is Agape, the Love of God. The enemy of God is the enemy of Love; fear is of the devil and is the enemy of Love.

There is no fear in love, but perfect love casts out fear, because fear has torment. He who fears has not been perfected in love. (1Jn 4:18 MKJV)

There is no torment with the Lord. With the devil however, he is a tormentor and an inflictor of pain. The Lord does not afflict His beloved children just as how a natural father will not torment or enforce pain on his children. The Lord chastises to bring correction and discipline it may be painful for a season but it is not affliction or torment. The devil enjoys affliction and torment because he is evil and it brings pain and suffering. Torment is what happens in hell.

And it came to pass, that the beggar died, and was carried by the angels into Abraham's bosom: the rich man also died, and was buried; And in hell he lift up

> his eyes, being in torments, and seeth Abraham afar off, and Lazarus in his bosom. (Luk 16:22-23 KJV)

King Jesus does not torment. In the earthly ministry of Jesus of Nazareth there isn't a point where we see Jesus tormenting anyone. He rebuked wickedness but never tormented people. He only warned of eternal judgment and torment for those who reject God. Remember to reject God is to reject Love. Whoever rejects Love accepts torment from the evil one over Love from God.

> That is the way it will be at the end of the world. The angels will come and separate the wicked people from the godly, throwing the wicked into the fire. There will be weeping and gnashing of teeth.
> (Mat 13:49-50 NLT-r)

It must be understood our Heavenly Father does not send anyone into torment in hell. Hell was made for the devil and his demons. People choose wickedness over righteousness. Wherever there is fear there is the works of the flesh and every form of evil. Wherever there is God there is the fruit of the Spirit which is Love and it's by products. As Saints we must choose Love over fear.

When someone is motivated by fear the result is evil. Why would someone lie about someone else? I've learnt lies will always be traced back to the spirit of fear. A person is afraid of someone getting ahead of them so will lie to bring them down. Alternatively a person may be afraid of being exposed for their own wrong doing so they lie attempting to cover their sins.

A colleague of mine was taught by his grandmother a truth I will share here. She said and I will quote her verbatim "a liar is a thief and a thief is a murderer". This saying may come from elsewhere, nevertheless it is true. All forms of wickedness stem from fear. The sprit that works in the devil is fear. Whenever he drives people to commit sin the driving force is fear. Child of God fear is not from within you, it is an outside force you must resist!

For God hath not given us the spirit of fear; but of power, and of love, and of a sound mind.
(2Ti 1:7 KJV)

We are born again and have the Spirit of God. This is a Spirit of Power, Love and a Sound Mind. Where there is fear there is no peace. With God we have a sound mind which is peace. Someone may ask what about the fear of the Lord? The bible tells us to have fear of the Lord. Let me explain.

And the spirit of the LORD shall rest upon him, the spirit of wisdom and understanding, the spirit of counsel and might, the spirit of knowledge and of the fear of the LORD; (Isa 11:2 KJV)

In this context the word fear, in "fear of the Lord" is reverence and respect for the Lord. It is not about being afraid because of possible pain, affliction or torment but respect because of honour for the Lord. Here is the word fear used in this verse above in the Greek.

H3374

יִרְאָה

yir'âh

yir-aw'

Feminine of H3373; *fear* (also used as infinitive); morally *reverence:* - X dreadful, X exceedingly, fear (-fulness).

Re; Strong's Dictionary

We must respect Christ with godly fear. Anything which comes to you that does not bring peace but brings torment is not of God. Any action which is not of Love and is of fear will lead to evil. We must cast out evil which is fear, with truth and Love.

But if ye have bitter envying and strife in your hearts, glory not, and lie not against the truth. This wisdom descendeth not from above, but *is* earthly, sensual, devilish. For where envying and strife *is,* there *is* confusion and every evil work. But the wisdom that is from above is first pure, then peaceable, gentle, *and* easy to be intreated, full of mercy and good fruits, without partiality, and without hypocrisy. And the fruit of righteousness is sown in peace of them that make peace. (Jas 3:14-18 KJV)

Act

Choose to embrace Love and resist fear.

The enemy of God is the enemy of Love; fear is of the devil and is the enemy of Love.

Love God Not Money – Day 37

No servant can serve two masters: for either he will hate the one, and love the other; or else he will hold to the one, and despise the other. Ye cannot serve God and mammon. (Luk 16:13 KJV)

The only thing which Jesus compared Himself with on earth was money. He did not compare Himself with wickedness or evil. In relation to serving and loving; Jesus only compared Himself with avarice, mammon that is the Love of money! Think about that. The main thing against serving God is serving money. To serve money is to Love money more than God.

For the love of money is the root of all evil: which while some coveted after, they have erred from the faith, and pierced themselves through with many sorrows. (1Ti 6:10 KJV)

The Love of money is the root of all evil! In the previous day we had the revelation that fear is the driving spirit of evil. This implies that all fear has the Love of money as its source. Therefore we can trace all works of evil to fear and the Love of money. This is clearly seen throughout the bible and if you haven't already learnt this in life you will see it openly. Anyone who is not truly serving Jesus is serving money.

When someone does not trust God it means they do not have faith in Him. A person who does not have faith in God has faith in something else. That something else is not of God. That something else is faith in fear which is nothing more than faith in the devil. From here people will serve money and put their trust in money. You may think man of God that is a bit of an assumption. No it is not. If someone is not serving God they are serving money. Why does someone steal? They don't trust God for provision. Why does someone lie or kill to cover their sins motivated by Love for money.

Solomon was the wealthiest king of his time and was led astray by his desire for strange women. It was a result of him serving his riches and not the Lord as he did when he began to reign. Judas was the treasurer in Jesus' ministry. He pretended to be serving Jesus but was actually serving money. Hear the words of Judas below.

Why was not this ointment sold for three hundred pence, and given to the poor? This he said, not that he cared for the poor; but because he was a thief, and had the bag, and bare what was put therein.
(Joh 12:5-6 KJV)

This led to Judas committing the ultimate wicked sin of betraying and selling the Messiah! Judas did not have faith in God his faith was in money. He was serving money all along. Any child of God who does not serve God with their resources and finances is serving money and does not trust the Lord.

Let me make it clear and simple. Any believer who knows they must pay tithes and offerings and chooses not to, is a servant of money and not God. Jesus gave the test of faithfulness towards Him with a test of faithfulness with money.

He that is faithful in that which is least is faithful also in much: and he that is unjust in the least is unjust also in much. If therefore ye have not been faithful in the unrighteous mammon, who will commit to your trust the true *riches?* And if ye have not been faithful in that which is another man's, who shall give you that which is your own? (Luk 16:10-12 KJV)

Jesus said whoever is unfaithful in money will not be faithful in the things of God. If you are a leader of a ministry take this wisdom. A test of the faithfulness of the people of God is their faithfulness in finances. Anyone who does not serve God with their money cannot be trusted. You cannot have a non-tithing leader, they are unfaithful. There is no compromise here. It is no coincidence that the very next verse after Jesus gave the test for faithfulness is the one below.

No servant can serve two masters: for either he will hate the one, and love the other; or else he will hold to the one, and despise the other. Ye cannot serve God and mammon. (Luk 16:13 KJV)

They hold unto the one. What do they hold unto?

Over the years in ministry I have seen this play out. A child of God, even leaders are so diligent in church work but not in their finances. Then they receive a job, a business breakthrough or increase in finances. From here their time in church is limited or their behaviour "seems" to change. Others are shocked at the absence or sudden change in a person. I am not because the test of faithfulness will always stand. In all their serving, if they did not prove their Love for God by serving Him with their resources they were never truly serving Him!

But those who have a desire for wealth are falling into danger, and are taken as in a net by a number of foolish and damaging desires, through which men are overtaken by death and destruction. For the love of money is a root of all evil: and some whose hearts were fixed on it have been turned away from the faith, and been wounded with unnumbered sorrows.
(1Ti 6:9-10 BBE)

Trust Jesus and serve Him. Whoever does not trust Jesus, trusts fear and serves money. The Lord desires to bless with wealth, riches and money in fact it is a reward of serving Him. Love God and have serving Him as your motivation, this will keep you away from the choking torment of the devil. For some receive money in unrighteous ways and become trapped.

And these are they which are sown among thorns; such as hear the word, And the cares of this world, and the deceitfulness of riches, and the lusts of other things entering in, choke the word, and it becometh unfruitful.
(Mar 4:18-19 KJV)

Love God, Love His commands, His ways and He will bless you, answer your prayers and set in a high place.

I love them that love me; and those that seek me early shall find me. Riches and honour *are* with me; *yea,* durable riches and righteousness.
(Pro 8:17-18 KJV)

Because he hath set his love upon me, therefore will I deliver him: I will set him on high, because he hath known my name. (Psa 91:14 KJV)

Act

Love and serve God with your resources and money.

Any child of God who does not serve God with their resources and finances is serving money and does not trust the Lord.

A test of the faithfulness of the people of God is their faithfulness in finances. Anyone who does not serve God with their money cannot be trusted.

Love Is The Greatest – Day 38

And now abide faith, hope, love, these three; but the greatest of these is love. (1Co 13:13 NKJV)

These three virtues of faith, hope and Love abide. They are available to believers and all three have their place. Faith is our trust and response to our belief in God. Hope is confidence for something good in the future. Love is God. Faith operates in the present tense. It brings results immediately. Hope is for the future. It keeps one unmoved. Love is for all times. This is one of the reasons why Love is the greatest because it works in all situations.

So these three things remain: faith, hope, and love. But the best one of these is love. (1Co 13:13 GW)

Faith has its place in receiving and living in the moment. We live by faith. It is an amazing virtue. With faith however you cannot wait for something to happen. Hope enables you to endure and wait. The two need each other. Faith is the evidence of what is hoped for. After hoping, faith receives what was hoped for. Faith is dependent on Love. Love is unique.

For in Jesus Christ neither circumcision availeth any thing, nor uncircumcision; but faith which worketh by love. (Gal 5:6 KJV)

Hope makes us unashamed because of the Love of God in us. Faith, Hope and Love all work together but faith and hope are reliant on Love. This does not mean that Love functions alone without faith and hope. They all work together. But just as with the fruit of the spirit all having Love as the base so it is with faith and hope. We can say Love is the source of faith and hope; so is greater.

In this book we have been looking deeply at what Love is and what it enables and does. Love is not proud but humble. Humility serves.

But he that is greatest among you shall be your servant. (Mat 23:11 KJV)

The disciples of Jesus got into a debate on who of them was the greatest. Interestingly the Lord did not rebuke them but told them how to be the greatest. The one who is the greatest servant is the greatest. It takes humility, patience and kindness to serve. These are attributes of Love. Jesus became the servant of all through His death on the cross.

Let this mind be in you, which was also in Christ Jesus: Who, being in the form of God, thought it not robbery to be equal with God: But made himself of no reputation, and took upon him the form of a servant, and was made in the likeness of men:
(Php 2:5-7 KJV)

Jesus humbled himself to be a servant. When Jesus washed the feet of his disciples he was fulfilling the duty of servants in those days. That is why Peter initially refused Jesus to wash his feet. Peter knew Jesus washing his feet was for a lowly duty of a servant.

[That] Jesus, knowing (fully aware) that the Father had put everything into His hands, and that He had come from God and was [now] returning to God, Got up from supper, took off His garments, and taking a [servant's] towel, He fastened it around His waist. Then He poured water into the washbasin and began to wash the disciples' feet and to wipe them with the [servant's] towel with which He was girded. When He came to Simon Peter, [Peter] said to Him, Lord, are my feet to be washed by You? [Is it for You to wash my feet?] (Joh 13:3-6 AMP)

This is one of the secrets of the Kingdom of God, serving. It is a reflection of the greatest, Love serves without motivation of a reward. Love does not serve for a reason other than Love. There is no because attached to serving other than because of Love. In the world people may serve to be seen or to earn promotion, favour or finances. That is not service driven by Love.

Servants, be obedient to them that are *your* masters according to the flesh, with fear and trembling, in singleness of your heart, as unto Christ; Not with eyeservice, as menpleasers; but as the servants of Christ, doing the will of God from the heart; With good will doing service, as to the Lord, and not to men: Knowing that whatsoever good thing any man doeth, the same shall he receive of the Lord, whether *he be* bond or free. (Eph 6:5-8 KJV)

Love is the highest level of excellence. Abraham the father of faith received the promises God gave him. The prophets in the past spoke and prophesied of things they did not even see in their lifetime. They spoke in faith and held on in hope that what they spoke would happen. Jesus Christ came and brought excellence and perfection, the fulfillment of all that came before him. He came as God to the earth, He came as Love, the greatest of all sent. Not as a servant of God but the son of God. Love is the greatest. In all things you do, let them be done in Love and powered by Love. By this you will achieve greatness like Jesus.

And after He had appeared in human form, He abased and humbled Himself [still further] and carried His obedience to the extreme of death, even the death of the cross! Therefore [because He stooped so low] God has highly exalted Him and has freely bestowed on Him the name that is above every name,
(Php 2:8-9 AMP)

Declaration

I declare that I will follow the example of Jesus and serve God with my life. I will allow God to work in me and do all things by Love in Jesus name. Amen

---

This is one of the secrets of the Kingdom of God, serving. It is a reflection of the greatest, Love serves without motivation of a reward.

Love Is Perfection – Day 39

Therefore leaving the principles of the doctrine of Christ, let us go on unto perfection; not laying again the foundation of repentance from dead works, and of faith toward God, Of the doctrine of baptisms, and of laying on of hands, and of resurrection of the dead, and of eternal judgment. (Heb 6:1-2 KJV)

Every Christian that is born again receives the Spirit of God, which is a Spirit of Love, Power and a Sound Mind. They must however grow up spiritually and renew their mind to live as the Lord desires. The Lord desires mature sons of God. Maturity is perfection.

You'd expect a child to make a lot of mistakes but not an adult. As someone grows as a child of God they have to feed themselves with the milk of the word of God. They must grasp concepts of salvation, faith, repentance, the new birth and the like. After this we move on and deal with the weightier matters of Christianity which is Love in truth.

But earnestly desire the best gifts. And yet I show you a more excellent way.
(1Co 12:31 NKJV)

The gifts of the Spirit are not perfection but still important. The Apostle Paul said desire spiritual gifts but there is a more excellent way. What is the more excellent way? It is Love. This is where in chapter thirteen it goes on to explain the attributes and operation of Love. This letter was to the church in Corinth, which we see was a carnal church that is it had a majority of baby Christians. They were immature in Christ they needed the gifts of the Spirit in order for God to work.

A mature child of God is not reliant on the gifts of the Spirit. They know how the Spirit of God works and flow with Him. Love is perfection. The purpose of faith, prophecies, tongues, miracles, healings, is to build up to Love. Jesus of Nazareth did not work through gifts; He worked through compassion which is Love. He did not wait for the Holy Spirit to come upon Him and move Him to heal the sick. He went about doing good healing all who were oppressed of the devil. He knew that's what Love does.

But when he saw the multitudes, he was moved with compassion on them, because they fainted, and were scattered abroad, as sheep having no shepherd.
(Mat 9:36 KJV)

The Apostle Paul had much opposition and betrayers some were Christians but Paul knew his mission was one of Love and he continued sharing the gospel. An immature Christian would've sought out justice and clearing of their name with the noble saints before continuing but Paul did not. He knew the works of the enemy and that the Lord justifies not man.

Therefore, as the elect of God, holy and beloved, put on tender mercies, kindness, humility, meekness, longsuffering; bearing with one another, and forgiving one another, if anyone has a complaint against another; even as Christ forgave you, so you also must do. But above all these things put on love, which is the

bond of perfection. (Col 3:12-14 NKJV)

Have you ever seen toddlers crying and fighting? When you wonder what all the crying is about you discover it's a very petty issue. One child won't let the other play with a certain toy or something like that. It's the same in life. Immature people will fight and squabble over petty matters. The mature are driven by Love. They use the Spirit of God to judge what or who is right or wrong in a situation. They then minister truth which comes with mercy, forgiveness and repentance.

But the natural man receiveth not the things of the Spirit of God: for they are foolishness unto him: neither can he know *them,* **because they are spiritually discerned. But he that is spiritual judgeth all things, yet he himself is judged of no man. For who hath known the mind of the Lord, that he may instruct him? But we have the mind of Christ.** (1Co 2:14-16 KJV)

A baby Christian will say; "don't judge let God judge". A mature Christian knows how to judge, they judge using the Spirit of God. Matthew chapter seven says don't judge but it speaks in reference to hypocritical judgment. This is where one has much wrong with themselves but condemns the actions of everyone around them. We must remove the log in our eye before checking the splinter in our brother's eye. You must judge matters. That is to be able to see what is righteous and unrighteous in any situation.

Do ye not know that the saints shall judge the world? and if the world shall be judged by you, are ye unworthy to judge the smallest matters? (1Co 6:2 KJV)

But solid food belongs to those who are of full age, that is, those who by reason of use have their senses exercised to discern both good and evil.
(Heb 5:14 NKJV)

Love keeps everything together in perfection. The enemy of unity can be immaturity or a bitter unrepentant heart. An immature child of God may be ignorant of certain matters so can be corrected. A mature Christian who is stubborn and refuses correction falls into the trap of the enemy.

It is important for Christians to grow up so that truth can continue. When there are baby Christians they can be deceived by a disobedient more mature Christian who tries to sway the baby Christians to follow them. In such cases the truthful mature one is seen as the enemy. Where there is ignorance false ministers thrive.

Till we all come to the unity of the faith and of the knowledge of the Son of God, to a perfect man, to the measure of the stature of the fullness of Christ; that we should no longer be children, tossed to and fro and carried about with every wind of doctrine, by the trickery of men, in the cunning craftiness of deceitful plotting, (Eph 4:13-14 NKJV)

Unity comes about through maturity in Love. The teachings made up by man will fizzle out and the word of truth will prevail. Whatever needs to be done in any life situation when dealt with in truth and Love will bring out the perfect Will of God.

God forbid: yea, let God be true, but every man a liar; (Rom 3:4a KJV)

The reason everything begins is to reach its full potential and expected end. Your life has an expected end. The expected end is not death but you becoming all that God created you to be. You being the perfect gift you were made to be by the Lord. Love is excellence.

But speaking the truth in love, may grow up into him in all things, which is the head, *even* Christ: From whom the whole body fitly joined together and compacted by that which every joint supplieth, according to the effectual working in the measure of every part, maketh increase of the body unto the edifying of itself in love. (Eph 4:15-16 KJV)

The Lord wants us to be perfect just like He is.

Be ye therefore perfect, even as your Father which is in heaven is perfect. (Mat 5:48 KJV)

Confession

I confess that I will pursue Love in all things. I will grow to be a mature child of God led by His Spirit in all things. I will grow to the fullness of the Christ in Jesus name. Amen

---

Whatever needs to be done in any life situation when dealt with in truth and Love will bring out the perfect Will of God.

God Is Love – Day 40

He that loveth not knoweth not God; for God is love. (1Jn 4:8 KJV)

In the previous thirty nine days we have expounded on Love. The pinnacle of the truth of Love is that God is Love. Languages can be limited in their expression this is why we have broken down the spiritual truth as to what Love is. It is more rather who Love is. There are many amazing characteristics of God. He is merciful, slow to anger, gracious, compassionate, holy, all powerful, all knowing, the creator, wisdom, the beginning and the end. All this is and more is summed up in God being Love.

And we have known and believed the love that God has for us. God is love, and he who abides in love abides in God, and God in him. (1Jn 4:16 NKJV)

The world has a wrong idea of who God is because they have a wrong idea what Love is. Similarly some believers have a wrong idea of who God is because they have no real understanding of Love. This book has been driven by Love to bring to light what Love really is and therefore who God really is.

God is not a judge waiting to execute judgment. Yet He still judges righteously. God is merciful and forgives yet He still brings justice. God is patient and kind yet He is not weak. God is slow to anger yet He can become angry. To know God is to know Love. From the introduction I made it clear that there are different types of Love and uses of the word Love in languages. True Love must be understood as the Love of God. It is unconditional and eternal. God will continue caring for people who reject Him. God's power is Love, something that cannot be understood by the world. How can you be kind to your enemy? How can you bless someone who curses you? How can you say give in order to receive? Love defies all the wisdom of this world.

For since in the wisdom of God the world through its wisdom did not know him, God was pleased through the foolishness of what was preached to save those who believe. (1Co 1:21 NIV)

Love is not proud. God is not proud. In order to get to know God you have to humble yourself. This is how Love works. The Lord protects what He has as precious from the proud. The more you can lower yourself down the more you will know Jesus and be lifted up.

Neither be ye called masters: for one is your Master, *even* Christ. But he that is greatest among you shall be your servant. And whosoever shall exalt himself shall be abased; and he that shall humble himself shall be exalted. (Mat 23:10-12 KJV)

As you Love God and Love yourself you will be able to Love your neighbour. There is a power which cannot be explained in natural terms that will come alive in you. Love is selfless, it casts out fear it casts out evil, it uproots all wickedness. Love is seen in actions. It is not just in mere talk but it proves itself not in a prideful way.

For scarcely on behalf of a righteous man will anyone die; yet on behalf of the good, perhaps someone

might even dare to die. But God demonstrates His own love toward us, in that while we were still sinners, Christ died for us. (Rom 5:7-8 CAB)

God demonstrated and proved what Love is through Jesus. To know God is to know Love. Whoever knows Love becomes Love. Study this book continually. Study the life of Jesus in the Gospels, look at His words and actions. This will change you greatly and lead you to become who your Heavenly Father called you to be.

My beloved friends, let us continue to love each other since love comes from God. Everyone who loves is born of God and experiences a relationship with God. The person who refuses to love doesn't know the first thing about God, because God is love--so you can't know him if you don't love. (1Jn 4:7-8 MSG)

Love always wins and completes the task.

When Jesus therefore had received the vinegar, he said, It is finished: and he bowed his head, and gave up the ghost. (Joh 19:30 KJV)

Act

Love God. Love yourself. Love your neighbour.

God demonstrated and proved what Love is through Jesus. To know God is to know Love. Whoever knows Love becomes Love.

Conclusion

The Gospel is a message of the Love of a Father, the Love of a King, the Love of God to us. As you grow in grace and the knowledge of Jesus Christ you will grow in Christ. As you do, you will be perfect just as your Heavenly Father is perfect. We have the nature of God in us. We have the capacity and ability to be perfect in all we do. We must learn how to use the Love we have.

Christians separate, divorce and stop associating together yet they will say the Love each other. A couple may truly Love each other but divorce. A child of God may truly Love his church and pastor but leaves the ministry. Why does this happen? It happens when people do not know how to function in Love. Their understanding of Love is limited. They are either unskilled or refuse to follow the Spirit of God. This book is filled with truth that will guide you to do what Love will do in every situation.

Humble yourself; desire to know Jesus and you will come out victorious. Love never fails. Child of God you will not fail as you choose to understand Love and obey Love. Of all the books in the forty days with God serious without a doubt this one is the most complete. If you read this book without going through the other six in this series, you will not get the revelation brought here in it's fullness. Love is perfection. Stay blessed!

Beloved, let us love one another, for love is of God; and everyone who loves is born of God and knows God. He who does not love does not know God, for God is love.
(1Jn 4:7-8 NKJV)

With Love & Blessings

Jason Pullen

Other Books by the Author

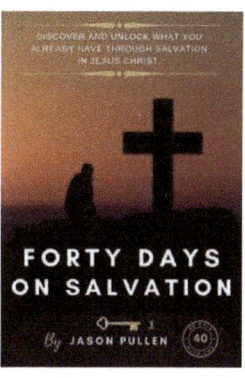

www.ingramcontent.com/pod-product-compliance
Lightning Source LLC
Chambersburg PA
CBHW062208080426
42734CB00010B/1845